SAILPOWER

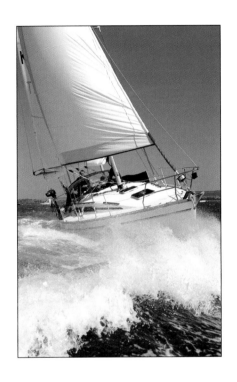

SAILPOWER

Trim and Techniques for Cruising Sailors

Peter Nielsen

S SHERIDAN HOUSE

This edition published 2004 in the United States of America by
Sheridan House Inc.
145 Palisade St
Dobbs Ferry, NY 10522
www.sheridanhouse.com

Note: While all reasonable care has been taken in the production of this
publication, the publisher takes no responsibility for the use of the
methods or products described in the book.

Library of Congress Cataloging-in-Publication Data

Nielsen, Peter,
    Sailpower : trim and techniques for cruising sailors / by Peter Nielsen.
        p. cm.
    ISBN 1-57409-177-8 (hardcover : alk. paper)
1. Sailing.   2. Sails--Aerodynamics.   I. Title.
GV811.N494 2004
797.124--dc22

                                    2004005841

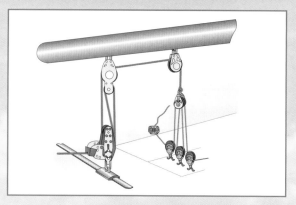

Design by Susan McIntyre

Printed in Singapore by Tien Wah Press (Pte) Limited

Contents

No two cruising yachts are alike and nor will their sails be trimmed exactly alike. The only way to find the optimum trim for your boat is to go sailing and practise, practise, practise.

Introduction

This book has its origins in a series of articles that appeared in *Yachting Monthly*. It had become apparent to us that a great many recreational yachtsmen either didn't know, or didn't care, about the finer points of sail trim. We thought it was a shame that many people weren't getting the full potential out of their boats, so we enlisted the help of John Channon, MD of Hood Sails, as our personal coach, and set to the task of demystifying sail trim and sail handling.

We found there were plenty of books available that majored on sail trim, but they tended either to be so crammed with physics and algebra that your eyes glazed over within a couple of pages, or they aimed squarely at racers; in the latter case most books presupposed that the boat had perfect sails and a full crew to do the tweaking. Either way, there wasn't much to draw in the typical leisure sailor with the typical cruising boat, equipped with sails that might be a little past their best, and possessing a hull shape that is not intended to knife to windward like an America's Cup racer.

That's where this book comes in. It's aimed at neither the total beginner or the total expert, but at everybody who, like me, fits in somewhere between these two extremes.

We have concentrated on practice, not theory. My treatment of the theory of sailing might be a little lightweight for some tastes; if you want page upon page of dense text, algebra and endless diagrams, there are plenty of other books that will give you those. But if you just want to know how to sail better, then read on.

Peter Nielsen

A handsome cruising yacht, with her sails perfectly trimmed to maximise her full potential, is a beautiful sight.

1 How Sails Work

Lift and drag

Apparent wind

The slot effect Under Bernoulli's Law, air is fluid. When it accelerates, pressure is reduced; when it slows, pressure is increased. Here, the airflow is compressed, which accelerates it in accordance with Venturi's Law and thereby reduces its pressure. The lower pressure on the lee side of the mainsail causes it to be sucked, or lifted towards the sail.

The best-known researcher into how sails work is C A Marchaj, who admits in *Sailing Theory and Practice* that the interaction between sails 'is still a controversial subject and not fully understood.' Indeed, it is a subject that is surrounded by various theories, many of which conflict to greater or lesser degrees, and each with its vociferous proponents. So if even an eminent scientist confesses that he can't get a solid grip on this subject, the rest of us can hardly be expected to comprehend every nuance. But rest easy – it really doesn't matter too much. Those prehistoric sailors who found that an outspread animal skin propelled their log canoes downwind couldn't have cared less about the aerodynamics of sailing. They would just have been grateful for a break from paddling. Even now, thousands of years on, it is far from necessary to understand the finer points of aerodynamics in order to trim your boat's sails, any more than you need a scientist's grasp of hydrodynamics to manoeuvre it under power. This is not rocket science. That's why I'm not going to attempt to delve too deeply into the theory. There are plenty of books around that will do that, and mighty dry reading most of them are too.

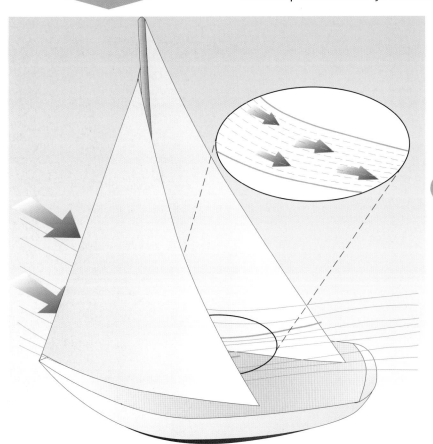

Lift and drag

Nevertheless, a grasp of the basic principles is important to understanding how trimming affects your sails. More than 250 years ago, a Swiss mathematician called Jacob Bernoulli worked out that when airflow speeds up, air pressure drops. Airflow accelerates over the curved surface of an airfoil, as in the leeward surface of a sail, because it has further to travel than that on the other side. The lower pressure on the leeward side of a sail therefore causes it to be sucked, or

Sailpower

lifted, towards the wind. You can try this theory for yourself by turning on a tap and holding the back of a spoon close to the stream of water. As the spoon approaches the running water, it will be sucked towards it because the acceleration of the air surrounding the water stream causes the pressure to drop as the spoon approaches it. Holding your hand out of the window of a moving car will also demonstrate this effect. If you

APPARENT WIND

Sails are trimmed according to the apparent wind, which changes in direction and strength according to how fast the boat is going and its angle to the true wind (A, B and C). You can work out how the apparent wind affects the boat on different points of sail. Draw a line (1) parallel with the boat's centreline. Its length

– say 1cm = 1 knot – represents boat speed. Line 4, to a similar scale, indicates the direction and strength of the true wind. Complete the parallelogram by drawing in lines 2 and 3. Connect the opposite corners of the parallelogram with line 5, which indicates the apparent wind direction and velocity.

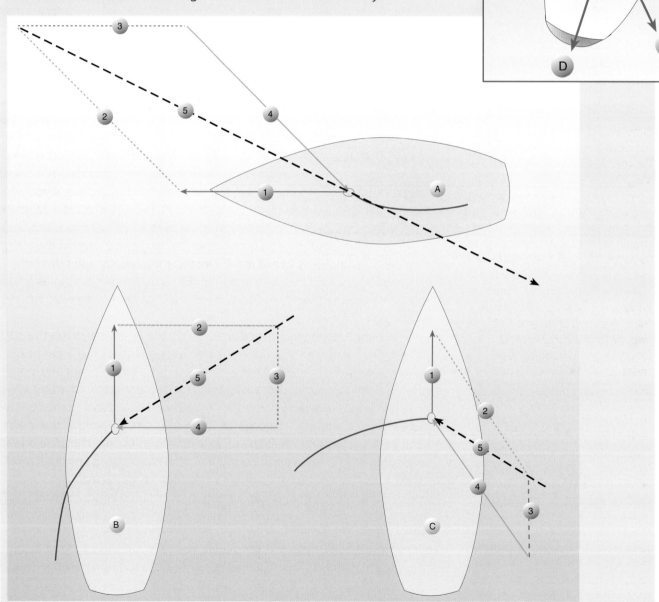

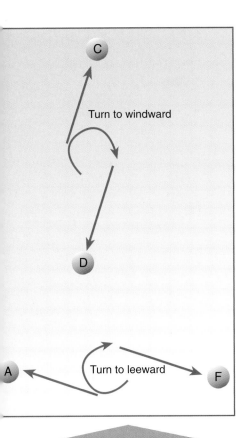

Here we see how a boat goes to windward under the influences of wind and water. The wind acts on the sails in two ways; it drives the boat forward and it pushes it sideways. The effect of water can also be split into two: longitudinal force, the hull's resistance to being moved forwards, and perpendicular force, its resistance to being moved sideways.

A is the lateral driving force of the wind. C is the longitudinal driving force. B is the combination of the two, or total driving force. D is the longitudinal resistant force, and E is the total resistant force. F is the lateral resistant force of the water.

As the hull is heeled when going to windward, the two longitudinal forces do not act along the same line, and they form a couple that tries to turn the boat towards the wind. At the same time, the lateral driving force on the sails and the lateral resistant force of the water also form a couple, but one which tends to turn the boat away from the wind. When these opposing forces cancel each other out, the boat will be balanced under sail.

hold your hand, palm downwards, edge-on to the wind and arrange your fingers and thumb to approximate a curved airfoil shape, you will find that your hand will be deflected upwards – you have generated *lift*. Lift, which acts at up to a right angle to the wind, is what makes a boat sail to windward. The opposite component of lift is *drag*. Drag acts in the same direction as the wind and 'pushes' on the sail. Which of these two parts of the total sail force is the dominant driving force depends on the angle at which the airflow meets the sail – its angle of attack.

Lift pushes the boat sideways and forwards. Drag will also push the boat forwards, but only away from the wind. To move satisfactorily to windward, the lift generated by the sails must be allied to that provided by the boat's keel, which, along with its rudder, is another airfoil shape. The sail force tries to push the boat sideways, which means the water flow meets the keel at an angle. Just as the airflow speeds up over the leeward surface of the sail, so the water flow accelerates over the leeward side of the keel, and the resulting pressure drop generates lift. When the boat is sailing downwind it doesn't make leeway, so the keel no longer generates lift; all the keel is does on that point of sail is to create drag over its surface – one reason why dinghy sailors lift their centreboards when sailing downwind.

That portion of the sail force which is not driving the boat forward and instead tries to push it sideways is called the *heeling force*. As the wind strength increases so does the thrust acting on the sails – and so does the heeling force. When going to windward, you try to make the twin airfoils of headsail and mainsail produce as much lift as possible while keeping the heeling forces to a minimum. The sails need to be positioned at the proper angle of attack to the wind in order to keep the airflow attached and generating lift. When the airflow becomes detached too soon, as a result of a badly shaped or trimmed sail, the sail 'stalls' and loses drive; if you look out of an aircraft window you can sometimes see this effect illustrated as the airflow curves over the top of the wing and breaks into turbulence as it nears the trailing edge. If it broke closer to the leading edge of the wing, the result would be a loss of lift. Oversheeting a sail has the same effect. The objective of sail trim is to keep the flow attached for as long as possible when going upwind, and to angle the sails to make drag work for you when going downwind.

The main and jib work together to guide the airflow through the gap or 'slot' between them. The headsail deflects air across the leeward side of the mainsail, increasing the pressure in the slot and slowing down the air flow. This drop in pressure brings the apparent wind around the mast forward, and allows the main to be sheeted in closer to the centreline than the headsail. The speed of the flow through the slot drops gradually as the headsail is sheeted closer to the main. When the speed over the lee side of the main is equal to the wind speed over the windward side, the slot effect is working at its optimum. As the jib is sheeted even closer, the flow through the slot becomes too restricted and pressure builds up on the lee side of the main, causing it to backwind and eventually stall. If the slot is too open, performance also suffers.

The slot effect makes the jib more efficient than it would be if it were working alone. It also makes trimming the sails a slightly more complicated task, because each sail has to be adjusted so that it complements the efficiency of the other.

2 The Rig

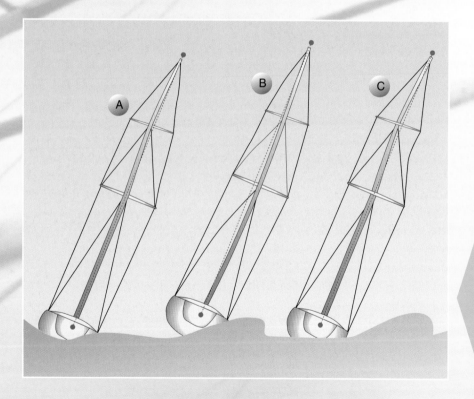

The more spreaders, the more awkward to set up. Here are some typical examples.
A – windward intermediate too tight.
B – windward lower too loose.
C – windward cap shroud too loose, windward intermediate too tight.

In a perfect world you'd be able to set up a mast so that it was held immoveably in any direction you could name – longitudinally, laterally, diagonally – and then walk away and worry no more about it. Unfortunately, yachts don't work that way. The mast and rigging might look simple enough, and the forces they have to contend with are no secret, but the relationship between them is not so straightforward. That's why you see so many sagging forestays and full-bellied sails every weekend.

With a little thought and a bit of work, the average cruising yacht will point higher, sail faster, handle better and generally give her crew a lot more pleasure – and that, after all, is why we go sailing. You can fiddle about with sail trim all you like, haul the boat out and scrape her bottom in search of that extra half-knot, but true sail power begins with a well-set up rig.

Setting up the rig

First, the rigging needs to be adjusted with the boat at rest so it's as upright and well-tensioned as you can get it, and then the rig needs to be fine-tuned; this can only be done under sail. To begin with, if the boom is still attached to the mast, either remove it or lower its end to the deck and slide the mainsail out of its track. This makes it easier to sight up the mast track.

Then slacken off all the bottlescrews sufficiently so that the mast is loosely supported. Usually, the shrouds are adjusted from the top down. Throughout the procedure, make sure you adjust each opposing shroud an equal number of turns.

Setting up the masthead rig

• The first step is to centre the masthead over the middle of the boat. Tighten the cap shrouds as much as you can by hand. Check for lateral straightness by freeing off the main halyard until it just touches the cap shroud chainplate on one side of the boat when under tension. Then take it to the opposite chainplate. If there's any difference, adjust the bottle-screws and re-check as many times as necessary. When the mast is vertical, as a rule of thumb, you can put two more full turns on each bottlescrew with spanners or a spike to reach a reasonable sailing tension.
• Next, harden up the backstay and forestay in the same fashion as the cap shrouds. This is when you will determine the amount of rake the mast has. It shouldn't be more than one per cent of the mast's height. Get the backstay as tight as possible; if it's too loose, the forestay will sag off. If the mast starts to bow forward, slacken off the forestay bottle-screw a little and take up on the backstay.
• At this point, adjust the intermediate shrouds if you have a double-spreader rig. Tighten them up by hand and then with spanners, making sure the mast remains straight athwartships, but leave them a little looser than the caps. Cap shrouds, being the longest wires on the boat, will stretch more and so need to be tighter.
• Tighten the fore-and-aft lower shrouds, or aft lowers and babystay. The lowers should be about the same tension as the cap shrouds.

13

Sailpower

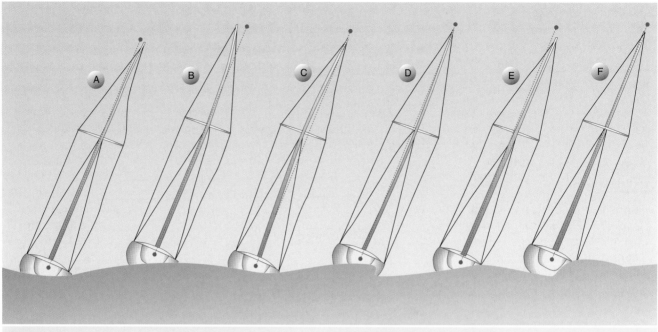

Setting up a rig can be a process of trial and error, but it gets easier with practice. Here are some typical problems with a single spreader rig.
A – windward cap shroud too loose.
B – windward cap shroud too tight.
C – windward lower too tight.
D – windward lower too loose.
E – cap and lower shrouds too loose.
F – perfection.

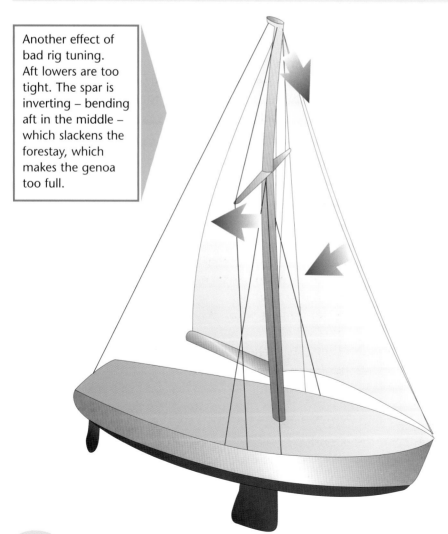

Another effect of bad rig tuning. Aft lowers are too tight. The spar is inverting – bending aft in the middle – which slackens the forestay, which makes the genoa too full.

SPREADERS

The importance of correct spreader angles is often misunderstood. A pair of spreaders which are horizontal is bad enough; if they're drooping below the horizontal plane then it's a matter of when, not if, you strike trouble.

The force applied by shroud to spreader, and therefore from spreader to mast, must always be horizontal, which is why the spreaders should bisect the angle of the shroud as it passes over the spreader tip. This invariably means the spreaders should be angled upwards a little. Cable clamps above and below the spreaders, or a tight seizing, will prevent them from slipping.

WHAT IS MAST RAKE?

When a mast leans towards the stern of the yacht it is said to be raked aft. The degree of rake can affect the balance of the helm. Too much aft rake will increase weather helm because the sailplan's centre of effort moves aft. Conversely, raking the mast forward will decrease weather helm. That said, on many yachts mast rake has more effect on appearance than performance – spars look better with a little rake.

Rake can checked by hanging a weight from the main halyard down to deck level and seeing how far from the back wall of the spar it hangs, or by eye from a few yards along the pontoon. To be on the safe side, never rake your mast back by more than its fore-and-aft diameter.

It is not unheard of for riggers, if they've cut a new forestay too short, to compensate by raking the mast forward. This makes the rig 'soft', more liable to bend in the wrong direction. It also makes getting decent forestay tension more difficult.

Why bend the mast?

Mast bend is a means of keeping the forestay tight and the sails flatter, mainly for improved performance to windward. Any pre-bend in the mast should take the form of a fair curve from partners to masthead. On a masthead rig, mast bend should be limited to one per cent of the mast's height. Half the fore-and-aft diameter of the mast is a good rule of thumb, but this can be exceeded with a fractional rig, which by its nature requires a bit more pre-bend. Mast bend tends to straighten out when the boat is sailing.

Fine-tuning

Now you're halfway there, and you need to go sailing to fine-tune the rig in, ideally, a decent force 3. Mast tuning follows a logical procedure. Basically, if any part of the mast is out of line, then you tighten up the shroud that supports the bit in question.

Put the boat hard on the wind and feel the lee rigging. As the windward rigging stretches, the lee shrouds should start to go slack at about 20 degrees of heel. If there's no slack at all in the lee shrouds then the rigging is too tight and should be freed off a little. The shrouds should not be waving around in the breeze, just loose enough that they can be deflected by hand.

Now sight up the mast track. If it is straight, then the adjustment is about as good as you're going to get it. Rigging wire will stretch under load, which means it is almost inevitable that the masthead will deflect a little to leeward in a strong breeze. The best you can hope for is to ensure that this deflection is smooth and well controlled, and that the middle sections of the mast are in column.

Tack the boat to perform any adjustments – if you tighten the windward bottlescrews under load, you may damage their threads – then tack again to see what effect your adjustments have had. Then check the rig on the other tack.

The shrouds should be tensioned equally on both sides, so keep count of the number of turns you put into each bottlescrew. Also remember that the aft lowers are used to straighten out lateral bends in the mast; the forward lowers/ babystay are there to stop the mast from inverting and to keep a slight bend in the mast.

As soon the opportunity occurs, check all this again when the boat is reefed. You may find that the mast is bending slightly aft in the middle, because the sail's leech tension is now acting on an unsupported section of the mast. Adjust the babystay or forward lowers to compensate.

Why it pays to check the mast carefully – this spreader could fail at any time and bring the rig down.

Sailpower

▲ Swept-back spreaders usually denote a fractional rig, but increasingly, masthead rigs also have them.

Fractional rig

The principles remain the same for fractional rigs, but setting these up can be tricky, especially on bigger boats. On a typical 7/8 (or thereabouts) modern fractional rig with swept-back spreaders, the cap shrouds provide all the forestay tension, while the backstay primarily functions as a tuning aid. Because these shrouds act in two planes, laterally and fore and aft, tightening them will push the middle of the mast forwards. In effect you are putting pre-bend into the mast section, and this is all that stops it from inverting, for fractional rigs do not have forward lower shrouds or babystays to counter the pull of the forestay. This means the aft lower shrouds must also be set up very tightly to limit the amount of mast bend as well as support the mast laterally.

• Leave the backstay slack. By hand, tighten the cap shrouds and forestay together until the desired mast rake is achieved and the mast is straight athwartships. Then wind them tighter with a pair of spanners, two turns at a time.

• Take up on the lower shrouds (and intermediates, if it is a double spreader rig) until they are hand tight. Then tighten up the caps and forestay some more.

• Tighten up the intermediates and lowers until the pre-bend is correct – about 0.5 per cent of mast height. You can measure this by hanging a heavy shackle from the main halyard and measuring its distance from the mast partners. Too much mast bend – much more than two per cent – will fatigue the spar and shorten its life. On a double-spreader mast, the lowers should be a little tighter than the intermediates.

NOT A LOT OF PEOPLE KNOW THAT...

• The mast step must support a compression loading of between one and a half and two and a half times the boat's displacement. Chainplates must be able to meet a loading more or less equal to the boat's weight.

• Sparmakers can make a mast stiffer by reducing the length of the unsupported panels (ie from mast step or partners to the spreaders). This is why we are seeing more yachts in the 10m range with double-spreader rigs. On the face of it, this makes for a more complicated rig, but it will be stronger and, because the mast section can be slimmed

16

Fractional rigs (left) are increasingly common these days and are usually marked by bigger mainsails, often with pronounced roach (A). They'll have plenty of pre-bend in the mast and rely on the cap shrouds acting on aft-swept spreaders to keep the forestay tensioned.

Masthead rigs have smaller mainsails (B) and less highly stressed rigs, usually with forward lowers or a babystay to prevent the spar from inverting.

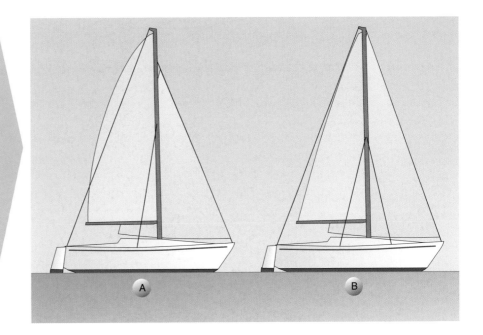

A   B

Tuning under sail

Because the shrouds have to be set up so tight it is difficult to fine-tune a fractional rig. The lee cap and lower shrouds should not be slack at all when the boat is sailing. If they are, then the mast is unstable and it is only a matter of time before it goes over the side. If you are in any doubt about how to set the mast up, hire a professional rigger to show you how to do it. It will be money well spent.

down as a result of the extra support, lighter.

• The wider the shroud base, the less stress on the mast and boat, but the less efficient the headsail sheeting angle. Moving the shrouds inboard also lets the headsail sheet tracks come in closer to the boat's centreline, which will improve windward ability. It also increases shroud loadings so the chainplates and hull must be strong enough cope with the extra stresses; a double spreader rig will be needed to make up for the steeper shroud angles.

• With a new boat, check the rig tune after a few hundred miles of sailing. The wires will have stretched and the rig will almost certainly benefit from adjustment.

• When initially setting up a mast, it helps to walk away from the boat and look at her bows-on from a distance. This will give you a better idea of whether the mast is leaning to one side.

• If, when tuning your rigging, the slack doesn't come out of the wire when you're hardening up the bottlescrews, you are in trouble. It means the structure of the boat has failed in some way; either the hull is flexing or the chainplate attachments are coming adrift.

• Although many rigs have stood for 20 years or more, riggers say you should think about replacing the standing rigging on a masthead boat after about ten years; earlier than that if you're going offshore. The consensus of opinion is that more highly stressed wires on fractional rigs should be replaced every five years.

• Don't be a tightwad and hang on to your existing forestay when fitting roller reefing. Furling gear puts different stresses on forestays and an old one could fail without warning.

Sailpower

Keel-stepped masts

The procedure for setting up a keel-stepped mast depends on whether the mast heel can be adjusted in its step. Make sure that the mast is centred in the deck aperture. Tighten the shrouds enough so that the spar is supported vertically, and centred laterally in the deck aperture. Sight up the spar to see if there is any forward rake in the mast; if there is, move the heel slightly forward – vice-versa if the mast is raked too far aft. If the heel isn't adjustable then you will have to set up the mast rake using the stays.

The mast will be held in place by hard rubber chocks. The wear marks on these will give an indication of how far to drive them in (of course, you'll have marked their positions when the mast was removed...).

HOW TO IMPROVE AND MAINTAIN YOUR RIG

• If re-rigging a boat for long-distance cruising, you could do worse than fit Norseman or Sta-Lok mechanical terminals, at least on the lower ends of the standing rigging. Corrosion is always much worse in lower terminals, where water and salt collect.

• Rigging wire is less prone to metal fatigue if it is articulated – free to move in more than one direction. Toggles must be fitted to all sail-carrying stays, and shrouds and backstay will benefit from them too. Make sure chainplate, bottlescrew, wire and mast fitting are all in perfect alignment.

• Never tape up the entire open body of a bottlescrew – always leave a gap at the bottom so water can get out. For the same reason, if you have those natty PVC covers, make sure they're open at the bottom. When it comes to your rig, seeing is believing.

• If you have plastic shroud protectors, make sure they don't rest on the top of the wire terminal. A surprising amount of dirt and salt collects in them, which will speed up corrosion.

• Go over swages and bottlescrews with a magnifying glass at the start of every season to look for cracks.

• Strip, inspect and grease your bottlescrews every year. Anhydrous lanolin is a good 'clean' lubricant.

• Don't be overzealous with a spike when adjusting bottlescrews – it can cause minute cracks in the body. Use spanners instead for the last turn or two.

• Don't use clevis pins that are too long or too thin. They'll always be a weak point in the rig.

• Never use split rings on a shroud or stay. They can work themselves free. Use the right size of stainless steel split pin, bend them back far enough not to snag sails, and apply plenty of tape.

• Resist the temptation to tie springs or other lines off on your bottlescrews or chainplates. It does them no good at all.

• Monel locking wire is often better on bottlescrews than split pins – neater, and not so likely to snag skin, sheets or sailcloth.

• The kindest thing you can do to your standing rigging is to wash it down with plenty of fresh water, as often as possible.

• If you are replacing your rig, consider buying bronze bottlescrews instead of stainless steel.

▲ *A tiny crack by this sheave box could soon become a large crack.*

They are less affected by fatigue, and don't suffer from galling – the heat generated when SS bottlescrews are being tightened, which can lock them solid. Bronze used to be much more expensive than stainless steel but the gap has now narrowed.

• If the mast is unstepped for the winter, remove the wires and coil them neatly. They can mark the mast if left resting against it. Don't leave spreaders attached to the mast – someone is bound to walk into them.

WHAT CAN GO WRONG?

Wire Stainless steel wire is strong and lasts forever – as long as it's not attached to a boat. Corrosion and metal fatigue are the factors which cut short rigging wire's lifespan. The high cyclic loadings of everyday sailing will eventually 'work harden' the wire and weaken it.

Wire almost never breaks anywhere except where it enters a terminal fitting. If even one strand goes then you're in for a new shroud.

Terminals More rigs fall down because of terminal failure than anything else. Swages have earned a bad name, and rightfully so – a swage can look perfectly fine, but can conceal locked-in stresses which are just waiting for the right moment to burst out – but they are more prone to failure in the high salinity and humidity of the tropics than in the cooler waters up north.

If your shrouds have older-style stemball fittings which attach them to the mast, these also earned a bad name in the past. Newer designs are better.

Bottlescrews These are expensive, which is why many people don't replace them at the same time as rigging wire. A shame, because they're also prone to sudden and costly failure, the weak points being the forks and threaded shanks. Fatigue and crevice corrosion are to blame.

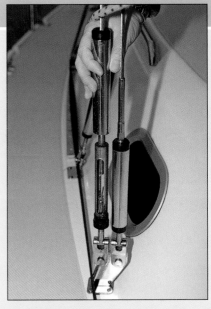

▲ *Covered bottlescrews are a mixed blessing – they look neat but can conceal a multitude of sins.*

◀ *Mechanical shroud terminals (above) can be disassembled for inspection; swage terminals (below) can fail without warning.*

Washing-up liquid will help to get them in; to ease matters, leave the wedges at the front of the mast until last, and then if necessary you can run a line around the mast from a cockpit winch, and grind in hard until you can get the last chock or two tapped into place. These wedges must not be tapered, otherwise they could work their way out.

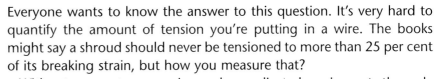

How tight is tight enough?

Everyone wants to know the answer to this question. It's very hard to quantify the amount of tension you're putting in a wire. The books might say a shroud should never be tensioned to more than 25 per cent of its breaking strain, but how you measure that?

Without access to expensive and complicated equipment, the only way to work out the loading on a shroud is to measure stretch. There are two easy ways to do this:

1 Put a little tension on the shroud and mark off a 2m section with tape. It takes about 5 per cent of the wire's breaking strain to stretch a 2m length of wire by one millimetre; therefore, if after tensioning your shroud there is now a 2005mm gap between your pieces of tape, your tension is 25 per cent of the breaking load.
2 Tape or clamp a 2m long batten to the shroud, with its lower end resting on the top of the rigging terminal. Tighten up your shroud, then measure the distance between the tip of the batten and the terminal.

Both these methods require exact measuring, but at least they're free. Bear in mind that it's impossible to stretch a length of stainless steel wire to breaking point by using normal hand tools to adjust the rig, but it might be possible to damage chainplate fixings. And, of course, if it becomes impossible to open or close doors down below, you have probably overdone things a little.

If you're unsure about how far to tension your shrouds, why not pay a rigger to come sailing with you for a couple of hours and show you how to do it? It would be money well spent.

WHAT KIND OF WIRE?

1 x 19 Almost every sailing boat is rigged with 1 x 19 stainless steel wire. This has a core of 7 strands inside a covering of 12 strands. It is very strong but not very flexible and can't be bent around tight angles.

▲ *This 1 x 19 rigging wire is showing its age; anything this rusty should be replaced.*

Dyform Stretches less than 1 x 19, and is stronger because more metal is packed into its strands. It's more expensive, and the nature of its construction – the strands are triangular in section – makes it hard on sheets and sails that rub against it. It can remove stitching in double-quick time and also wears hanks out more quickly. Dyform's low stretch means that

it can be used in smaller sizes than 1 x 19.

Rod Rod rigging is common on racing yachts but rarely seen on cruising yachts, for which its attributes of very low stretch and high tensile strength aren't really necessary. The price gap between rod and wire has narrowed recently but cruising people are still suspicious of it because it can fail without warning.

7 x 19 This flexible wire should never be used for standing rigging. It's for halyards and running backstays.

7 x 7 A stretchy, very flexible wire, best suited to low-load applications like guardwires.

Running rigging
A halyard obviously has to hoist a sail but it also has to make sure that the head of the sail stays where you want it to be. If the head sags then the shape of the sail will be affected. This why many cruising yachts have wire halyards, usually with a rope tail spliced on.

For halyards, 7 x 19 wire, with its 19 strands of 7 wires apiece, is the best bet. It's stronger and more flexible than 7 x 7, which means it can be run over smaller sheaves. A wire halyard's sheave should never be smaller than 20 times the wire diameter (double that for 7 x 7).

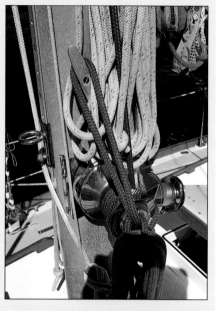

▲ *Low-stretch rope halyards are ubiquitous on today's cruising boats.*

All rope manufacturers now have prestretched braids that are suitable for halyards. Make sure you specify when buying the rope that you want it for halyards and not for sheets, though. Even prestretched halyards will get sloppy over time and if efficiency is important then they should be replaced every few seasons.

Expensive synthetics like Kevlar and Spectra are increasingly being used (always sheathed for UV and chafe protection), and offer excellent strength-for-size ratios. Kevlar doesn't take kindly to being bent sharply or kinked, which means it has to be spliced rather than knotted.

3 Sailcloth

Polyester rules, OK?

High-tech sails

At the beginning of the 1900s, most sails were made from Egyptian cotton which, not all that long before, had edged out the flax fibres which had been almost universally used for centuries. Polyester, which forms the basis of most sails today, was developed in 1941 by two British chemists. DuPont bought the rights to the invention for the USA, ICI for the rest of the world. It's DuPont's name for polyester yarn, Dacron, that's virtually become the generic name for the fibre.

Americans Lowell North and Ted Hood were among the first to adapt and refine polyester for sailmaking. Stronger and less stretchy than cotton, polyester took over the industry in a very short time.

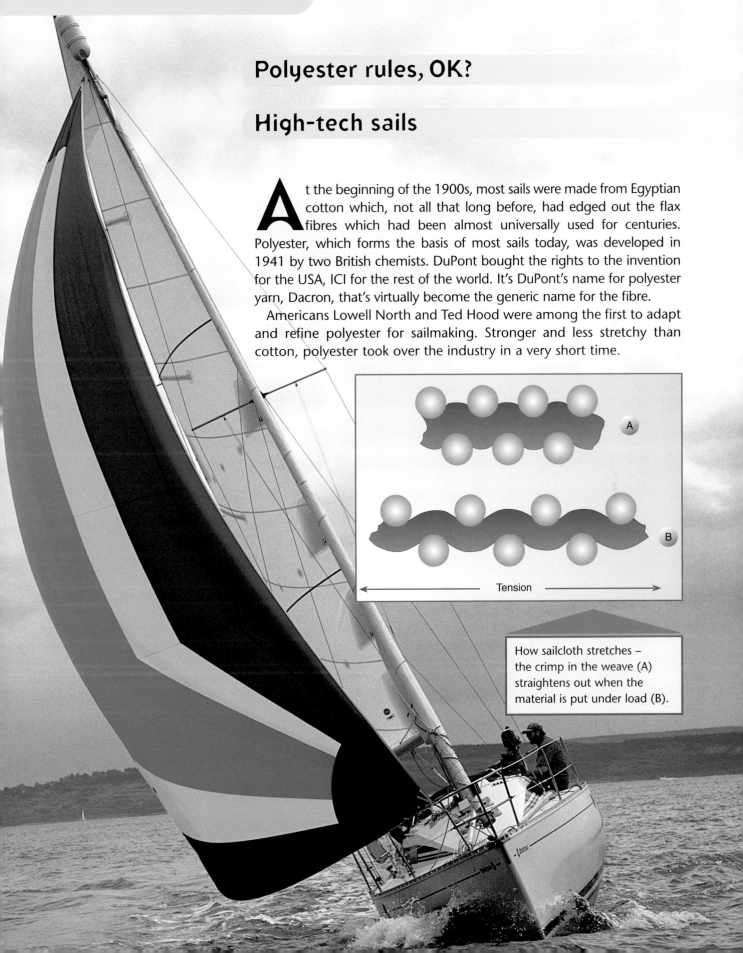

Tension

How sailcloth stretches – the crimp in the weave (A) straightens out when the material is put under load (B).

Sailpower

The ideal cruising sailcloth has minimal stretch, great strength, is resistant to dirt, abrasion and sunlight, is highly chafe-resistant, and won't absorb water. It should handle wind ranges greater than it was designed for without losing its shape, and positively enjoy other forms of mistreatment. It should also last the life of the boat.

Of course, such a cloth doesn't exist (if it did, the sailmaking industry would probably keep it under wraps!). There are some pretty good compromises around, though. To get an idea of the factors affecting sailcloth it's necessary to take a quick look at its physical properties and the terminology that describes them.

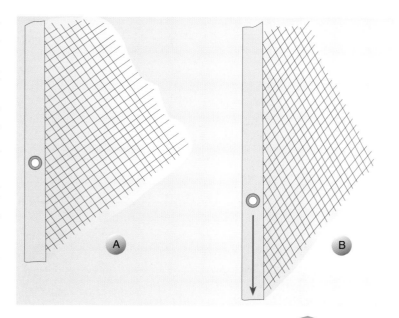

Sailcloth will stretch more on the bias to the weave – that is, at a 45 degree angle to the warp and fill (A).

When tension is applied on the bias (B) the cloth stretches and the sail changes shape.

Polyester rules, OK?

A woven polyester cloth has threads that run at right angles to each other. The *warp* is the lengthwise thread in the sailcloth. These threads are placed on the loom and then the *weft* or *fill* thread is passed back and forth through them. The density of the weave is controlled by beating the fill closer together. *Denier* describes the weight of the yarn. *Crimp* is the way the threads bend as they overlap one another. The *bias* is a 45 degree angle to the warp or fill. A *scrim* is a light, open-weave cloth used in many laminated sails.

The sailmaker will orientate the panels in a sail so that loads come on either the warp or the fill, because the fabric will stretch more on the bias. This can be demonstrated by pulling on the diagonally opposed corners of a handkerchief. The cloth can be made stronger in one direction than the other. Warp-oriented cloth has stronger threads running the length of the bolt. The most stable cloths have equal-strength threads running in both directions and are called balanced cloths. Analysis of where the forces act on a sail determines the type and orientation of the cloth used. Different weaves are used for different sails.

After the cloth is woven, it is often impregnated with a resin to fill the gaps between the fibres and improve stretch resistance, especially on the bias. The trouble with this is that after a season or two, much of the resin will have been flogged out of the sail. Some recently developed polyesters can achieve high stability without recourse to resins but they are more expensive. Finally, the sailcloth will be heat-treated to shrink the fibres and make them pull closer together.

It's common to use weights to describe the cloth grade. The named weight often bears little relation to the cloth's actual weight, due to variations in manufacturing. There is no official testing process for sailcloth, so manufacturers can claim anything they want.

▷ *Some sails last for 20 years or more, some just a few seasons*

Sailpower

High-tech sails

Most cruising sailors are quite happy with woven Dacron sails. They last for years, are easy to handle, cheap to maintain, and provide a level of performance that is entirely adequate for coastal, offshore or blue-water sailing. At the same time, many sailmakers are reporting increasing demand for high-performance laminated cruising sails. There is obviously a growing number of people who appreciate the edge that high-tech sails can give their boats.

Warp factor

No matter how high the fibre quality or how sophisticated the weave process – and this is constantly being refined – the nature of its construction means that a woven sail is eventually guaranteed to lose the shape that the sailmaker so carefully built into it. The warp yarns in sailcloth are run over and under the fill and adopt a crimped shape. The crimp will tend to straighten out progressively as the sail is under load up. No matter what the quality of the fibres or the weave, crimp remains the weak link. Also, because the load-bearing fibres run at right angles to each other, woven cloth is inherently unstable across the bias – at a 45 degree angle to the warp and fill yarns. Sooner or later, through the combined effects of wind, sun, flogging and general use, the crimped fibres will start to creep, and the straight fibres will begin to stretch.

A sail is built with its maximum depth (draft) forward of its midpoint for an efficient airflow. As the cloth degrades the draft will move aft and the sail will generally become baggier in its after sections. At this point the sail is 'blown out'. Depending on the cloth quality and the way the sails are treated by their owners, this process can take many years or just a few months. Many sailors scarcely realise their sails are worn out, or maybe don't care a lot; they still get where they're going and so what if the boat doesn't go to weather too well? To others, especially cruiser-racers who like to mix it up around the buoys, the loss of a sail's performance edge is not tolerable; it is to these people that sailmakers pitch their non-stretch, high-tech sails.

Laminate technology

Back in the 1970s, enterprising sailmakers began gluing polyester fabric to sheets of Mylar, a strong, flexible polyester film developed by DuPont originally for the packaging and food handling industries, Those early laminates were fast and efficient but far from durable – 'you could see the film peeling off the Kevlar during a race,' recalls one cloth manufacturer. But the potential was plain to see – the Mylar provided stability in all directions, allowing fewer fibres to be used, and eliminating the creep problem inherent in woven cloth.

Early laminated sails were little more than a loosely woven 'scrim' glued to one side of the Mylar substrate. The cost and fragility of these sails might not have meant much to well-heeled racers who thought

WHO NEEDS LAMINATES?

Much of the R&D leading to the current generation of cruising laminates was driven by the superyacht market. As rig technology developed to allow ever loftier spars to be put on ever longer sailboats, it became imperative to keep weight aloft to a minimum. Woven cloth simply can't offer the necessary mix of light weight and high load-bearing capability on bigger boats, and still be expected to keep its shape. That said, only a minority of cruising sailors will be able to justify the extra expense of laminated sails.

Someone with a performance-oriented boat of 40ft or more, who enjoys the occasional race and is fixated with sailing efficiently at all times, will see a real benefit from laminated sails. For the average cruising boat there is not much point except on yachts of 50ft or longer, when there might be gains from the lower weight and better shape-holding of laminated sails, especially with in-mast furlers. Some sailmakers suggest that even smaller cruisers would benefit from a laminated headsail, since jib shape is more critical than mainsail shape; a laminated roller-reefing head-sail is much less likely to suffer from shape distortion when it is partly furled.

One problem that the cloth manufacturers haven't overcome is that laminated sails are very susceptible to mildew. Their construction traps water and airborne dirt which in turn attracts fungus. In warm, humid climates, a cruising headsail rolled around a furling gear provides an ideal breeding ground for mildew. It won't affect the sail's strength, but who could stand looking at an ugly, discoloured sail, not matter how well it holds its shape?

◀ *Performance-orientated boats will benefit from laminated sails. Dacron is perfectly adequate for most cruising yachts.*

nothing of replacing them for every regatta, but they were not acceptable to cruisers. Thankfully, things have changed. The new breed of laminates is held together with advanced adhesives that have largely relegated delamination to an occasional, rather than regular, occurrence. Kevlar is still prevalent in racing sails but new fibres have been developed which are far better suited to cruising.

The cost and complexity of laminates vary according to the materials. Basic cruising laminates might consist of a light, woven polyester 'taffeta' cloth bonded to one or both sides of a Mylar film, usually over a load-bearing polyester scrim. Here the taffeta merely protects the film and scrim. These are not much more expensive than top-of-the-line woven sails. The next step is to make the scrim of PEN (Pentex) fibre; more expensive and durable still is Spectra/Dyneema, and right up at the top are the more exotic fibres like Vectran, Kevlar or Twaron, or carbon. Cruising demands other properties besides the great strength and stretch-resistance of these expensive materials. Ease of handling, user-friendliness and durability are important qualities for a cruising sail. Many of today's laminates are vastly more tolerant of being folded, flexed and rolled up around furling headsails, though few will withstand the kind of abuse that woven sails can handle. And although most fibres – polyester included – will eventually break down in sunlight, UV blockers and/or dyes added to glues and films give a high degree of protection.

Cloth manufacturers like Bainbridge, Contender and Dimension/Polyant each have their own brand names for cloths that, to the laymans' eye, differ only in small details. For example, most of the high-end-laminates now have fibres running across the bias as well as in the warp and fill directions. There is a general trend toward using flat ribbons of fibre in the scrims rather than rounded yarns; this slightly reduces thickness and improves the adhesion to the film.

The main differences between racing and cruising laminates lie in the fibres used. For most dual-purpose sails, the cloth makers will generally recommend yarns like PEN or Spectra. These do not have the high modulus or ultimate breaking strength of the aramids and others, but this is far from essential for most cruising applications.

Cloth makers continually mix and match the fibres in an ongoing search to combine their best points; carbon has been paired with Spectra, Kevlar with Vectran, polyester with Spectra, and so on. Building a high-end sail is a complicated process not unlike laminating a sophisticated composite boat hull; both procedures need top-quality materials and share the problems inherent in making dissimilar materials adhere to one another.

If the type of fibre used has a direct influence on the longevity and performance of the sail, so does the way it is oriented on the film. A basic scrim provides good support in the warp and fill directions while the Mylar prevents stretch on the bias. But Mylar can deform under extreme load, so much research has gone into orienting the fibres to follow the direction of the stresses on the sail. UK's Tape Drive, North's 3DL and Doyle's D4 sails are all variations on this theme which have successfully been adapted for cruising as well as racing over the last 10 to 15 years.

FIBRES FOR LAMINATED SAILS

Polyester
The rugged workhorse of sailmaking for nearly half a century, polyester fibre has it all – or nearly so. Depending on the quality, which varies widely, it is inexpensive, reasonably strong, and very durable. It is widely used in laminated sails, usually as a barrier cloth to protect the vulnerable film or load-bearing fibres.

PEN
Also known as Pentex, PEN fibre is of the polyester family but has twice the modulus, or stretch resistance, of a high-grade polyester. Its ultimate breaking strength is virtually identical. Originally developed for the automotive tyre industry, it has similar flex characteristics to polyester, so it stands up well to cruising use and abuse. It is an excellent fibre for laminated sails, especially for sub-40ft boats where weight saving is not a big issue.

Some cloth makers also combine PEN with high-grade polyester in woven sails. It is substantially cheaper than the more exotic fibres.

Dyneema

This polyethylene fibre is also known as Spectra. Its great strength, high modulus and proven durability makes it one of the most widely used high-tech sailmaking fibres. Spectra is virtually unaffected by flex and stands up well to ultraviolet light, which makes it ideal for cruising sails. Although not as light as the aramids or carbon fibre it still offers more than adequate weight savings for bigger boats. It has a tendency to creep under sustained loads, which is why it is not used in high-end racing sails. Cheaper than aramids, it is substantially more expensive than polyester.

Aramids

Developed for the automotive industry, Kevlar was one of the first fibres to be used in laminates back in the early 1970s. Twaron and Technora are other aramids used in sailmaking. Aramids have a high modulus and are massively strong for their weight. Sails made with them are very light but far from durable in a cruising context; Kevlar is brittle and does not stand up well to flogging and flexing.

Aramids have poor resistance to UV or abrasion, and laminates using them are limited to racing applications where durability is not a requirement.

Vectran

A liquid crystal polymer (LCP), Vectran is a high-strength, high-modulus fibre with some excellent characteristics that make it well suited to cruising sails. It stands up well to flexing and folding and resists chafe. It does not have Spectra's tendency to creep under load but nor does it have that fibre's resistance to UV degradation. Special coatings have been developed to protect it from sunlight.

Carbon fibre

Harnessing the properties of carbon fibre has been something of a holy grail for the sailcloth industry. It is immensely strong, very light and almost impervious to UV degradation, but it has been prone to sudden and spectacular failure in applications where it is subjected to repeated bending and flexing.

Carbon sails have proved fast and shapely, but they have gained a reputation for being fragile and short-lived. Development recently has centred on using flat, untwisted ribbons of lower-modulus carbon within a flexible coating that bonds to the laminate glue while allowing the fibre to 'float' within it. This vastly improves the material's capacity to cope with flexing and results have been promising enough for several sailmakers to start marketing carbon sails.

PBO

This the best-performing fibre developed to date, at least in terms of strength. It is used for standing rigging on Open 60s and America's Cup boats and has been used in top-end racing sails with varying degrees of success. Its biggest problem, apart from its high cost, is that it is extremely light-sensitive. Cloth manufacturers have resorted to dyed films, glues and taffetas in attempts to overcome this weak point, but it is unlikely that PBO will feature prominently in sails designed purely for cruising.

▲ *Kevlar sails are fast, fragile and best enjoyed by racers.*

Cost and durability

There is no doubt that laminated sails are more expensive to make than woven sails. The construction process is more complicated, as is the actual building of the sails. Radial cuts are favoured because the panels can be oriented along the stress paths of the sail and these cost more to produce. Low-end polyester/Mylar laminates are, say the manufacturers, perhaps 20 per cent more expensive than high-end woven cloth, but the price differential increases substantially with more exotic fibres.

There are two sides to the durability issue – ultimate lifespan, and ultimate performance. Today's laminates are far more durable than those of a just a few years back, but they can't match woven cloth for longevity. It's not unusual for woven sails to last 10 years or more, while the lifespan for a laminated cruising sail is closer to five years. The difference is that the laminated sail will still be setting well right to the end of its life. North Sails say a cruiser should expect around 2000 hours' use from a laminate against, say, 5000 for a woven sail. That doesn't sound much, but at, say, 10 hours' use each weekend for 20 weekends a year, it's still a potential 10 years' worth of stretch-free sailing.

4 The Headsail

Design

Headsail cut

In the relationship between headsail and mainsail, it's the headsail that wears the trousers. It meets the wind first and so its shape and trim are crucial to the functioning of the sailplan as a whole. To windward, it's probably twice as efficient as the mainsail. It doesn't have a nasty spar to disrupt the airflow along its leading edge, and it benefits from the wind directed on to it from the lee side of the mainsail. Because only one side of a headsail is fixed, it is not so easy to trim and tune as a mainsail, and therefore its design can make or break a boat's windward performance.

Design

There are two basic ways to build shape into what would otherwise be a flat, triangular piece of cloth. One is to cut a convex curve into one or more of the edges of the sail. When one of these curved sides is fixed to a mast, the excess material lends shape to the sail. Shape is built into headsails by broadseaming; basically, this is simply cutting a curve into a side of a piece of sailcloth, then sewing the curved edge to the straight edge of another piece of cloth.

Until comparatively recently the sailmaker's art was just that; a craftsman's eye, combined with trial and error, was reponsible for transforming a two-dimensional piece of cloth into an efficient airfoil. Computers have removed most of the trial and error and all the big lofts now design their sails on Cadcam programs. Sail panel shapes are plotted and cut by computer-guided machines. A sailmaker can change and refine the airfoil shape infinitely before the sailcloth has even arrived from the mill.

▶ *A well-cut and well-trimmed headsail is the key to efficient windward performance.*

Sailpower

Draft

This is the most important factor a sailmaker takes into account when designing a headsail. It gives the sail its power. Draft is determined by camber, which is the shape, or fore-and-aft depth, built into the sail. When the sailmaker decides on the camber, he also determines the point of maximum draft – the deepest point of the sail. This point will be a percentage of the chord, an invisible line running from luff to leech. As a rule of thumb, the camber will be between 40 and 50 per cent back from the luff. With the camber, the sailmaker tries to maintain an even windflow pressure between the windward and leeward sides of the sail; he aims to make sure the airflow across the sail will not break away until it reaches the leech. If a headsail is too full towards the leech, then the windflow, which does not like sharp curves, will break away much sooner on the leeward side. The resulting vortex, a spiral of air, lets the pressure to windward create extra fullness in the sail, compounding the problem. The boat heels more and slows down, which is the opposite of what you want.

The amount of camber in a headsail varies, with 8 per cent considered a flat headsail, 12 per cent a deep sail. Camber is always relative to chord length, and tends to be exaggerated in sails for smaller boats; these may have as much as 20 per cent camber.

Proportionately, more camber is built into the top of a sail, where the chord length is short; this part of the sail would otherwise be too flat and lack power. With most headsails, you will see the camber increasing slightly as you look up the sail, with least camber being built into the lower panels.

Entry angle

This is the angle of attack presented to the wind by the sail's leading edge. Entry angle also affects the location of the draft in the sail. With a fine entry the draft will be aft, with a full entry the draft will be forward. Generally speaking, the finer the entry, the higher the boat will point; the fuller the entry, the more power it will develop to windward. The boat's design has a large influence on the entry angle designed into a sail. A hull with a fine entry, which is designed to point high, will need a sail with a fine entry – as long as it is sailed in flat waters, where it is easy to steer the boat well. In big seas, where it is hard to steer a straight course (or when you are steering to the seas) the same boat will need a sail with a fuller entry, effectively moving the draft forward and giving the sail a wider 'groove'. In these conditions, pointing ability isn't as important as keeping the boat moving and maintaining the power to punch through seas. To sum up, a fuller entry makes for a more flexible and forgiving sail; one that won't require instant reaction to every windshift. Therefore it's a better all-round choice for those millions of us who aren't top racing helmsmen. The sailmaker will decide what entry angle your headsail should have, based on his experience of the type of boat and the conditions in which it will be sailed. Most cruising genoas are built with a fairly full entry angle.

▲ *This picture shows the amount of camber in a genoa trimmed for light airs.*

HEADSAIL CUT

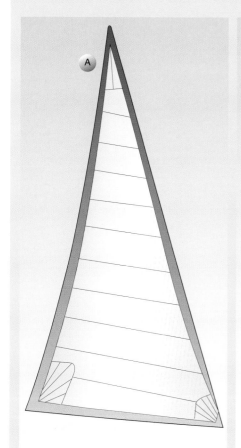

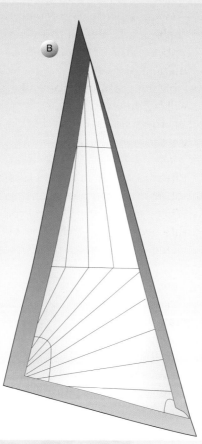

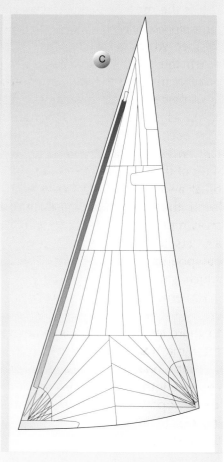

Headsail cut follows both fashion and technology. There are two types in favour today – crosscut and radial cut. The crosscut (A) has its panels running horizontally across the sail and parallel to each other. It needs a fabric with high strength in the fill direction.

The bi-radial sail (B) has panels radiating from the head and the clew and meeting at around the mid-point of the sail. This needs a warp-orientated cloth, as does the tri-radial sail (C). This has panels radiating from each corner of the sail, aligning the warp of the fabric with the heavy loads running from the tack as well as the head and leech.

Sailmakers were pushing radial cut-sails for all they were worth during the early '90s; they look sophisticated and sexy, and indeed must be used with laminates. For polyester, though, their virtues are often outweighed by cost and complexity. They are most often seen on performance cruisers, but their slight performance edge is wasted on the majority of cruising yachts. Still, yachtsmen who own performance cruisers, and perhaps like to race as well as cruise, will definitely see some benefit from the superior shape-holding of a laminated radial-cut sail.

Sailpower

Exit angle

This is the angle at which the wind flow leaves the sail. This relates to sheeting angles; the further inboard the sheet tracks, the wider the exit angle of the air flow. Too open an exit angle affects pointing ability; if it's too closed (leech curved too far to windward) the headsail will back-wind the main as the wind increases and slow the boat.

◁ *It is unfair to expect a single headsail to perform equally well on the wind and off the wind.*

Overlap

The bigger the overlap of the headsail, the closer the interaction between it and the mainsail. More overlap increases the slot effect. Overlap is calculated by dividing LP (luff perpendicular, a line drawn at right angles to the luff through the clew) by J, the length of the fore-triangle base. If J is, say, 12 feet, and the LP is 18 feet, then a 150 per cent genoa would have 6 feet of overlap.

There are three elements in measuring headsail size:

luff perpendicular (LP) is the distance to the clew from a right angle at the luff; J is the length of the foretriangle base; and the overlap is the amount by which the sail exceeds J – a 150% genoa is 1.5 times J.

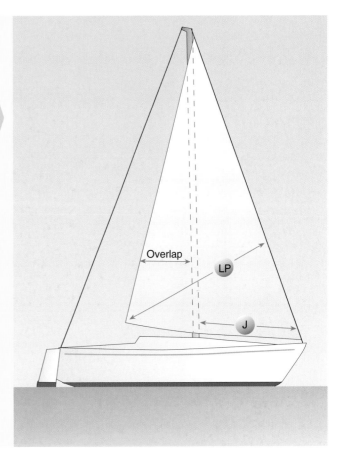

△ *There is a trend towards rigs with high-aspect ratio, non-overlapping jibs and large mainsails.*

Aspect ratio

This term describes the height of the sail relative to its area, or the luff-to-foot ratio. An overlapping genoa is a low aspect ratio sail; a tall and narrow blade type jib has a high aspect ratio. Designers of performance yachts favour high-aspect headsails because the long luff lengths give relatively high lift and low drag, making them efficient to windward. They are also easier to trim and handle, with less sail to sheet in when tacking.

A non-overlapping jib would seem to negate the slot effect theory, but the thinking is that the high-aspect sail permits a closer sheeting angle which 'cheats' the wind into treating the jib and main as a single airfoil, and so no slot is required. As pointing ability is relative to the luff length of the sail, the high aspect jib comes into its own wind range much sooner than a low-aspect genoa reefed to no. 2 size. An overlapping headsail is better in a seaway, though, where the narrow upper sections of the high aspect sail lose power quickly as the boat moves over the seas.

5 The Mainsail

Construction

Shaping the sail

Draft

Twist

Entry angle

Roach

Shelf foot

Battens

The fully battened mainsail

No battens

Controlling the main

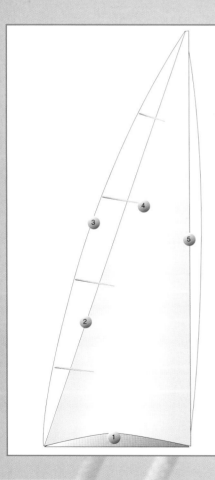

◀ **The elements of mainsail cut:** (1) foot and (5) luff curves are where extra material is added to give the sail shape; the roach (3) is the extra cloth outside the straight line from clew to head (2); battens (4) are necessary to support the roach,

▶ **Mainsail shape:** Not all panels are cut the same on a mainsail. At the foot (1), the panels are quite flat to decrease lift and cut down on drag. At the middle (2) there is noticeably more shape, while in the top third, the sail is made as deep as possible for increased power.

The mainsail is a complicated beast. It might not be as aerodynamically efficient as the headsail, but it's much trickier to trim and shape. Where you only have the halyard and sheets to fiddle with on your genoa, the mainsail suffers from a surfeit of influences: mast bend, halyard tension, outhaul, cunningham, foot shelf, boom vang, mainsheet, all these have greater or lesser parts to play.

Construction

Compared to a genoa, the mainsail on a bermudian-rigged yacht has a high aspect ratio; it is shorter on the foot and longer in the luff. The loadings imposed on the sailcloth by the wind will run from the clew to the head of the sail, whereas on a low-aspect ratio sail the loads will radiate from the clew towards the middle of the sail and curve towards the head. Hence different types of cloth are needed for mains and headsails.

On a crosscut mainsail the loads will be aligned in the fill direction, at right angles to the run of the sailcloth, and therefore the cloth needs a tighter weave across the fill to control those loads. You might think that the panels on the average crosscut mainsail would be cut to present a right angle to the mast, but the panel orientation is determined by the threadline, an imaginary line running from the clew to the head of the sail. The loads run along this line and so the panels are aligned to run at right angles to it, meeting the mast at a slight angle instead. Sailmakers will position the clew and tack reef points so that the loads stay aligned with the threadline as far as possible.

The vast majority of cruising mains are crosscut, and there are good reasons for this. A radial-cut dacron mainsail is fine, until it is reefed. Once that happens the loads are off the threadline and the cloth distorts. Enormous reinforcing patches have to be put in around the reef points and even then it's not uncommon for radial-cut dacron mains to blow out around the reefing cringles. As with headsails, radial cuts are best employed with high-tech laminated cloths and you're still far more likely to see them on racing yachts than cruising boats.

A fractionally-rigged yacht, with a higher proportion of its total sail area in the main, will have a mainsail of lower aspect ratio than a masthead yacht, but the sail is still built to the same principles.

▲ *A typical modern cruising mainsail; cross-cut and fully-battened.*

Sailpower

Shaping the sail

Like the genoa, the mainsail is more than a triangular piece of cloth. The sailmaker has to build or 'mould' shape into it, by a combination of broadseaming (cutting the seams with a slight curvature) and by putting convex curves – extra sailcloth – into the luff and foot. In this way he can determine the flow characteristics of the sail. Once the sail is hoisted and the luff and foot are stretched out straight on their spars, the extra material creates fullness in the sail.

The amount of luff curvature depends on the type of rig the boat carries. A bendy spar needs a fuller sail, because when the backstay is tensioned, the centre of the mast will bend forwards, taking the surplus cloth with it and flattening the sail. Mast bend isn't a big factor on the average cruising yacht so the cruising mainsail will tend to be cut fairly flat for better efficiency in moderate to heavy wind.

Draft

The mainsail's draft or camber – its depth – is measured in the same way as that of a headsail and is just as critical to its performance. It determines the amount of lift. Camber is expressed as a percentage of the chord (the distance from luff to leech) at any point on the sail; for example, 10 per cent camber indicates a flat sail, 20 per cent a rather full one. The point of maximum camber will be between 40 and 50 per cent back from the sail's leading edge.

Because the bottom quarter of a mainsail is aerodynamically less efficient than the upper sections, it needs to be flatter. Progressively more camber is built in towards the middle and head of the sail. The middle section of the sail generates most lift and power, and while there is too little area at the head of the sail to supply much lift, the camber is deepened to make the most of it.

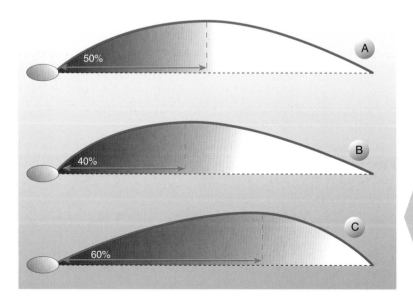

Draft positions
In a mainsail, maximum draft should be about 50 per cent aft (A) for normal sailing conditions. Tightening the halyard will move the draft forward (B) to around 40 per cent, which is desirable in heavier airs; if the draft is as far aft as in (C), the sail is probably stalled.

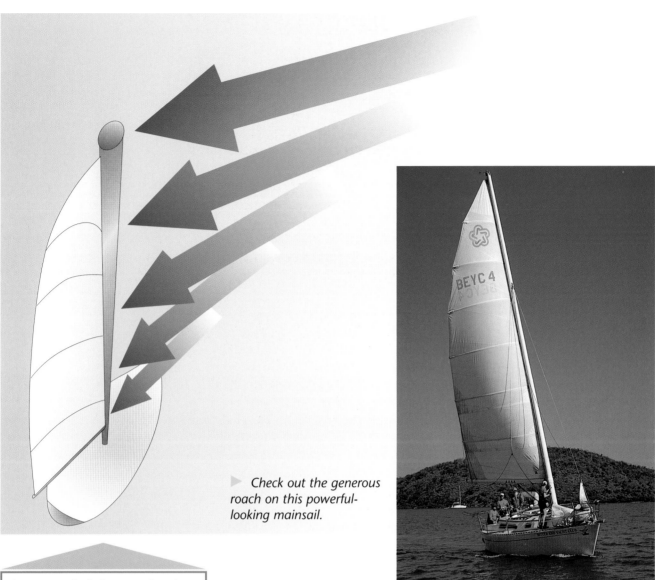

Check out the generous roach on this powerful-looking mainsail.

Apparent wind changes direction which is why twist is built into the top sections of sails.

Twist

The wind you experience at sea level isn't the same as that experienced at the masthead. It's slowed by friction over the water and so its velocity increases with height. Along with the change in speed comes a change in direction; the apparent wind at the masthead will be coming from further aft than that at deck level. This 'twist' in the wind has to be allowed for when the sail is being built.

Entry angle

The entry angle, or angle of attack presented to the wind by the sail's leading edge, is nowhere near as big a factor in a mainsail as in a head-sail. The mast effectively ruins the airflow at the sail's luff. It doesn't seem to matter whether the mast section is round, square or oval, the effects are the same. The air separates from the mast, creating a dead area at the leading edge of the sail, which is the main reason why the main is less efficient than the headsail. For all the good it does, the first foot or two of the mainsail might as well not exist. Indeed, furling gear maker Profurl claims that its wind tunnel tests prove this, which is one reason why the sail track for its in-boom furling system is separated from the mast section by several inches. The wing masts seen on many racing multihulls are an attempt to clean up the airflow over the front half of the sail and thus gain a little more speed.

Roach

This is the curvature in the leech of the sail. There are sound aerodynamic reasons for giving this part of the sail an elliptical form. An ellipse is the most efficient shape for an airfoil and a triangle is the least efficient. Elliptical shapes like aircraft wings suffer least from induced drag, the spillover of high-pressure airflow from the sail's windward side to the low-pressure on the leeward side, which has a braking effect. Mainsail roach is taken to its extreme in racing multihulls. So, given that elliptical equals fast, why don't headsails have roach? A genoa with an elliptical leech supported by battens would be lovely to behold, but it would foul the mast on every tack. Nevertheless, the headsails with a little roach supported by short battens are increasingly common on racing boats. The amount of roach on monohull mains is limited by the fact that they have to clear the standing backstay, while racing multis are more likely to rely on running backstays.

Shelf foot

Found on all racing mainsails and quite a few cruising sails, the shelf foot is an extra 'bag' of material built along the foot of the mainsail. When the outhaul is eased, as it would be in light airs or going downwind, the shelf foot provides a useful bit of extra sail area and adds shape to the foot of the sail. When the outhaul is tensioned, the shelf tightens up and flattens the lower part of the sail.

The shelf foot, shown here with the outhaul eased, adds a fuller shape to the lower part of the sail off the wind.

A typical 1970s-style high-aspect ratio mainsail; it needs all the roach it can get.

Battens

A batten's job is to support the roach in the sail and stop the leech from curling over on itself. There are typically four battens in the average mainsail, and this is a hangover from rating rules which restricted their number as well as their size. A batten is hardly a glamorous object but do not think that any old piece of wood or plastic will do. It has an important role in controlling sail shape and has to be rigid enough to support the roach while pliable enough to conform to the camber of the sail. Not so long ago, hickory was the favoured wood for battens, but now they're made from many different synthetics and to many degrees of stiffness.

The fully battened mainsail

There are those who hold that full-length battens have been the biggest development in cruising mainsails for decades, and it's difficult to argue the point. They're nothing new in the great scheme of things – the Chinese have used them on junk sails for centuries. First seen on multihull sails to support their extreme roach, they've been quick to catch on with the monohull contingent. Some lofts say that fully-battened sails account for as much as 80 per cent of new mainsail orders.

Once set up by the sailmaker, full-length battens lock the shape into the main across the entire chord, and better shape equals improved performance. The airfoil shape remains much more constant and it's not so likely that the draft of the sail will move aft as the wind increases. Being more forgiving, FB (fully battened) sails are much easier to control for those of us who aren't instinctive racing sail trimmers. They've taken a lot of the black art out of getting the best from a sail. Because they stop the luff of the main from backwinding when close-hauled, they remove the temptation to oversheet the main. The extra roach gives the FB sail more power, though the sail is usually cut a little flatter than a short-battened main and so is probably not quite so efficient in light airs; the stiffness and weight of the battens will conspire against achieving the ideal light-airs fullness. FB mains really come into their own in medium to heavy airs and are great for power reaching, as they are more efficient off the wind than short-battened sails.

Full battens have other benefits. They stop the sail from slatting annoyingly in light winds and flogging violently when reefing, easing both the nerves of the crew and the wear on the sail; because they don't flog they're easy to hoist and hand, and when combined with lazyjacks or a Dutchman system they'll rattle down on top of the boom without drooping all over the coachroof.

Of course, there are disadvantages too. The fully-battened main costs more to make and to perform at its best it needs some expensive hardware at the front end, where compression loads force the batten pockets towards the luff groove on the mast. Normal slides tend to jam and make the sail difficult, sometimes impossible, to hoist or hand, unless the boat is head-to-wind. This can make putting in or shaking out a reef a real chore. Fully-battened sails are awkward to stow unless the battens are removed. Sailing downwind, the batten pockets are more likely to chafe

◄ The fully-battened mainsail is commonplace these days – it offers many advantages, and some disadvantages.

▲ INSET To perform at their best, fully-battened sails need low-friction luff cars to absorb the loadings from the battens.

against shrouds. There's more weight aloft than with a short-battened sail. As with just about every aspect of boats, what you get is a compromise, but for most people the advantages of fully-battened mains far outweigh the negative points. It's also useful to know that a tired old main can be rejuvenated by having full-length battens retrofitted.

No battens

Mainsails cut for in-mast furling can't have battens, hence there is no roach, and must be built with a concave or hollow leech. Battenless sails aren't confined to mast furlers, though. Wary of the problems associated with battens, some blue water cruisers have their mainsails cut with a hollow leech. They happily trade some performance for an easier life – less maintenance on the sail, less weight, no problems in mid-ocean with broken or lost battens. Some Mediterranean charter fleets have also moved to battenless mainsails, and find them more forgiving for less experienced sailors – they spill the wind faster when overpressed, and the smaller sail area can be carried longer without the need to reef.

Controlling the main

There are so many ways to influence the shape of a mainsail that it can be a little off-putting. Here's a quick reminder:
- **Backstay** This controls mast bend, and is used to flatten the sail as the wind gets up.
- **Kicking strap** Used off the wind, this stops the boom from lifting, which leads to excessive twist.
- **Outhaul** It pulls the clew aft and tightens the foot of the sail.
- **Traveller** This controls the sail's angle of attack to the wind and balances the boat.
- **Mainsheet** It affects angle of attack and sail shape.
- **Cunningham** Used to cope with luff tension in the lower third of the sail.
- **Halyard** Affects luff tension and the location of the draft in the sail.

▶ *A good mainsheet arrangement and a powerful kicker are essential tools.*

6 Headsail Trim

The aim when trimming headsails is to adjust their aerodynamic shape and angle to the wind in order to obtain the best possible performance from the boat in the prevailing wind strength and sea conditions. Correct sail trim is most important when beating to windward, when the sails have to produce their maximum drive to overcome the resistance of headwind and seas. There is a dramatic difference in performance between a boat on which the sails are trimmed correctly and one where the crew has simply hoisted them and hoped for the best. When beating against a strong wind and steep seas, that difference could be a matter of one boat making progress and the other slipping back due to excessive leeway.

Sail trim isn't an exact science; there's a fair bit of art to it. None of the guidelines that follow are absolutely hard and fast, because there is so much difference between individual boats. The oldest trimming tip in existence, and one that applies equally to slow, heavy cruising boats and sharp cruiser-racers, is this: ease the sail until it starts to luff, then sheet it in until it just stops luffing. Even if you never bother taking your sail trim any further than this, it is a rule of thumb that will carry you a long way. But it won't give you that extra edge in performance that comes with using all the tools at your disposal to get your boat going as well as it possibly can.

Sailpower

Shape control

Because it is fixed along only one of its edges, the headsail is not as easy to trim as the mainsail. There are four ways of controlling its shape: Halyard tension, forestay tension, sheet tension, and sheet lead position.

Halyard tension

This affects the location of the draft in the sail. The ideal is to keep the maximum draft between 40 and 50 per cent back from the luff. As the wind increases, the draft will tend to move aft. Hardening up on the halyard will move it forward and create a fuller entry to the sail, which will increase power at the expense of pointing ability. Conversely, in light airs, easing the halyard a little will create a finer entry which will help the boat.

Backstay tension

Sail shape can also be affected by backstay tension. On the wind you need a tight forestay to flatten the sail. A sloppy forestay will sag even more as the wind gets stronger, thus making the sail even fuller and moving the draft aft, which is the last thing you want. The boat won't point as high and it will heel more. Some forestay sag is inevitable in any rig, no matter how well set up it is. On a masthead rig, fitting a backstay adjuster will go a long way to improving the situation. Before adjusting the backstay, ease the genoa halyard a little, or you'll be fighting against it. On a cruising fractional rig, backstay tension will tend to bend the mast rather than harden up the forestay, which is supported by the cap shrouds; it is usually not possible to tension the cap shrouds enough to take all the sag out of the forestay. A sagging forestay is actually desirable in light airs, when it makes the sail nice and full so it develops more power.

Adjusting trim Whenever you trim one sail, the other is affected to some degree. especially when the wind is forward of the beam. Oversheeting the headsail (1) causes the main to backwind, which leads to the mainsail being oversheeted until the luffing stops. Result – a slow boat. As the wind builds, it's often better to come off the wind a few degrees and ease the headsail to open the slot (2); this will allow you to ease the main down the track a little to lessen weather helm. As you come further off the wind (3) the headsail sheet lead should be moved forward; as the sheet is eased, the lead will naturally move outboard a little, which opens the slot more. This in turn allows the mainsail to be eased further without stalling (losing airflow).

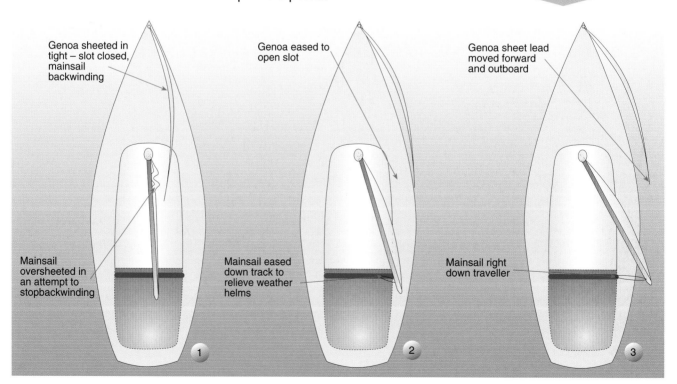

Genoa sheeted in tight – slot closed, mainsail backwinding

Genoa eased to open slot

Genoa sheet lead moved forward and outboard

Mainsail oversheeted in an attempt to stopbackwinding

Mainsail eased down track to relieve weather helms

Mainsail right down traveller

Sheet tension

Your most powerful genoa control is sheet tension. Once the halyard tension and sheet leads have been set up, trim in the sheet and the sail clew will move inboard, the leech will tighten and the sail will flatten. Trim the sheet until the genoa's leech parallels that of the mainsail in shape. On the wind, the last few inches of sheet tension are vital and will make a noticeable difference to the boat's performance as the sail is flattened and the draft is moved forward. If the main starts to backwind, ease the sheet a little to open up the leech of the sail. Sheet tension also has an effect on twist: the sail's built-in tendency to have its top half setting at a wider angle to the boat's centreline than its bottom half.

Sheet lead position

This is very important, yet is often neglected by cruising sailors. Most cruising boats have their genoa fairlead fitted to a track which allows its fore and aft adjustment. The importance of sheet lead in controlling twist and maintaining a proper headsail shape is often underestimated.

There is an ideal sheet lead position for every change in headsail area, and there's a simple way of determining this position. Remove the headsail and spread it out flat. Measure the luff length and mark the halfway point. Stretch a piece of line between this point and the clew, and use it as a reference point for a trim line – use indelible marker pen or sailmaker's tape – extending two or three feet from the clew.

As long as the sheet forms a straight line with the trim line, the genoa car should be in its optimum position for windward work. When the sail is reefed, and vice versa, the car can be moved until sheet and trim line are once again in alignment.

▼ *A trim line provides a good guide to sheeting angles. Here the lead is too far aft.*

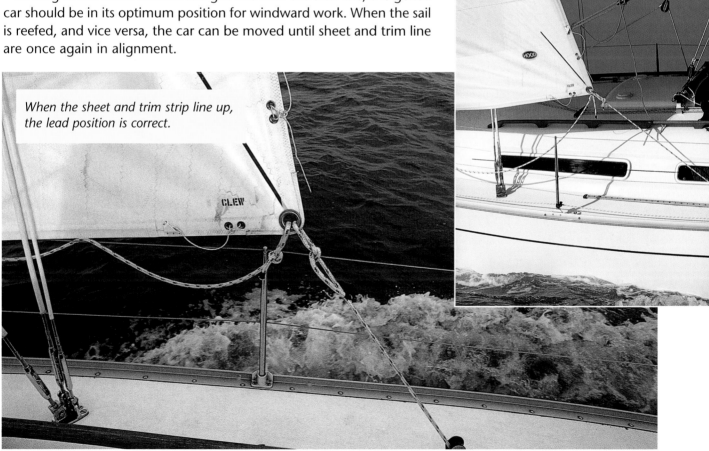

When the sheet and trim strip line up, the lead position is correct.

Sailpower

If the sheet lead is not moved forward when bearing off to a reach, the top of the sail will lose power.

By moving the sheet lead forward, the twist is taken out of the sail and it draws all the way up.

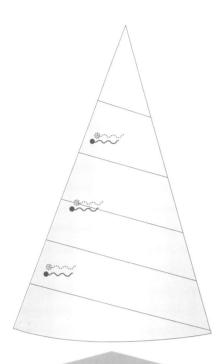

If your genoa doesn't have telltales, fit some right away. Position them at a quarter, halfway and three-quarters up the luff of the sail. They are the most important headsail trimming aid.

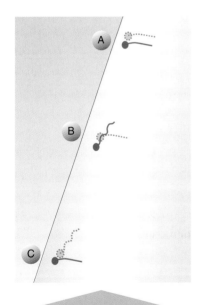

How to read telltales:
A Both streaming aft – perfect;
B Windward one breaking – sailing too high;
C Leeward one breaking – sailing too low and the sail is stalled.

As a rule of thumb for windward sailing, sheet leads should go forward in light airs, which slackens the foot of the sail and makes it fuller for more power. As the wind increases, the lead is moved aft to a position where there is more or less an even pull on leech and foot. If the wind keeps increasing, you can move the lead further aft, which lets the top of the sail twist off and spill wind.

As the sheets are eased to put the boat on a reach, the sheet lead should come forward to induce the proper sail shape, again using the trim line as a guide. One thing to watch: when the sail is eased well out, as on a broad reach, the trim line will give a false reading because the sail's clew will be so high, so if you get the lead as far forward on the track as possible you won't be far wrong. Used in conjunction with luff telltales, the sheet lead position is vital to assuring good windward sail trim.

Telltales

Telltales are a helmsman's best friend, and they're cheap too; all you need is a needle and a length of wool. Most headsails have three sets of them, evenly spaced along the luff of the sail at about quarter, half and three-quarter distance. They will tell you what's going on with the airflow across your sail, and provide the best indicator both of how well you are steering, and how well your sail is trimmed. Sailing to windward, if the genoa has been trimmed in correctly and all three sets of telltales are streaming straight aft in unison, the boat should be pointing high and sailing fast. If the leeward telltales break, then the sail is stalled and you need either to ease the sheet or steer up to windward until they stream aft again. If the windward telltales break, you need to come off the wind a few degrees or trim the sheet in some more.

Telltales are also a good guide to correct sheet lead position on a reach. When the sheet is cracked for a close reach, the top of the sail twists off to leeward. The bottom two windward telltales, which are usually all the helmsman can see, might be flying perfectly but the top one will be all over the place. It is are telling you that there is too much tension on the foot of the sail, not enough on the leech, so the top of the sail is luffing first. The remedy is simple: move the sheet lead forward. If the bottom windward telltale flutters first, the leech is too tight and the foot is too loose, and you should move the sheet lead aft.

Having the telltales offset slightly, so those to port are an inch or two higher than those on the starboard side, will make them easier to read. Making them different colours also simplifies reading them. They should be about five inches long, and located where they can't get hung up in the stitching of a seam. It is also a good idea to tie telltales to the shrouds and backstay – either light, thin ribbon or cassette tape work well. These will flow in the direction of the apparent wind, and are especially useful when sailing downwind, or at night, when you might not be able to see the wind indicator at the masthead.

No two cruising yachts are exactly alike and nor will their sails be trimmed exactly alike. The only way to find the optimum trim for your boat is to go sailing and practise, practise, practise.

Sailpower

▲ *Although telltales are flying correctly, the sagging forestay is giving the sail a fuller shape; backstay tension is called for.*

▶ *How the sail should look when sailing to windward in medium airs; note the difference in the camber stripes, which indicate the draft location.*

The effects of twist can be clearly seen here as the sail is eased off on a close reach

We are on a reach and there is too much twist in the sail. Bring the lead sheet forward until the top telltales stream aft.

Moving the draft

As a rule of thumb, you should aim to keep the flow, or maximum draft, in the headsail between 40 and 50 per cent back from the luff when going to windward. As the wind increases, the flow will tend to drop back to or beyond, the 50 per cent mark. In lightish airs and in flat water such a shape gives the sail a finer entry and allows the boat to point a little higher.

But as the wind increases, if the draft is too far aft the sail will be too full in the leech. The windflow will break away sooner on the leeward side, which lets the pressure on the windward side create even more fullness in the sail. The end result? The leech hooks to windward, creating

Sailpower

ROLLER REEFING GENOAS

The days when every cruising yacht had its forepeak stuffed with damp sailbags are gone, never to return. Tens of thousands of yachtsmen have never sailed a yacht with hanked-on headsails (and most have no wish to). On the average modern cruiser, one furling genoa has to do the work of three or four hanked sails, and to operate over a wind range of 5 to 35 knots; it's a lot to ask of a single sail.

Typically, a furling genoa will have between 130 and 150 per cent overlap. Progressively it can be rolled away to areas equal to a No. 2, 3, and four jib. Some sailmakers mark the reefing points along the sail foot – for a 135 per cent genoa, these would be at around the 115, 100 and 85 per cent tack points.

If the sail is simply rolled up around its luff, the extra material will belly out as the sail is furled, creating a very full shape in the middle sections, which is the exact opposite of what's desired in heavy airs. The result is an aerodynamic nightmare, a boat that won't point and is overpowered by the full sail, making lots of leeway.

To get round this problem, many sailmakers will build a long crescent-shaped piece of foam into the luff of the sail so that more cloth is rolled around its midsections, thus progressively flattening it. Some furling gears have independent head and tack swivels and will take up a couple of turns in the middle section of the sail before taking up the head and tack. If there is not some way of removing the belly, then a sail cannot truly be described as 'roller reefing'.

Ideally, the sail's clew will be cut high enough so that the helmsman can see underneath it. A secondary benefit is that the sheet leads do not need to be changed much when a high-clewed sail is reefed.

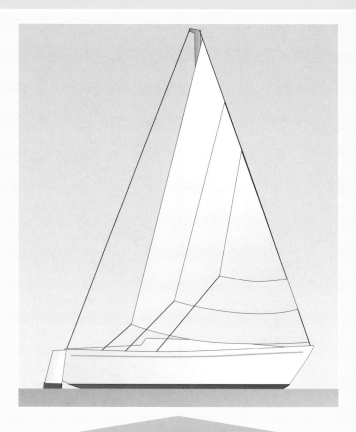

As a roller furled headsail is reduced in size, the sheet lead must be moved forward to keep the sail in its correct trim. It is not unusual for production boat builders to skimp on the length of the genoa tracks, with the result that it is impossible to move the sheet leads far enough forward when the sail is well reefed.

drag, and the boat slows down and heels more, making more leeway. It's like driving a car with the handbrake on.

The draft also needs to be moved forward, giving the sail a fuller entry, in livelier conditions where it is difficult to steer a straight course. In a seaway, pointing ability is not as important as keeping the boat moving and giving her the power to punch through the seas. Adjusting the sail's shape to maintain the windflow further forward, and sailing a few degrees lower, will make life much easier for the helmsman. Off the wind, draft location is not as crucial, as the wind pressure on the sail is not so readily translated into heeling forces.

It's difficult for the untrained eye to gauge the location of draft in a sail without the aid of camber stripes, which run from luff to leech and provide an instant visual reference. They're a useful and inexpensive modification.

▶ *Note the twist in this partly reefed genoa – the sheet lead needs to be moved forward.*

▶ This genoa does not have a foam luff, which is one reason why it sets so badly when partially reefed. There's no way of getting the belly out of the sail.

Sailpower

TRIM TIPS

Don't oversheet

A genoa winched in so hard that the spreaders are poking into it and the leech is stretched over the shrouds is a horrible, but sadly not uncommon, sight. It's also an inefficient way to sail. If the sail is sheeted in too flat for the wind angle, it will stall – the windflow becomes detached and the sail loses its lift. The boat will be slow and cranky, heel more, and sag off to leeward. In light airs, it may even stop dead. Telltales will point out the error of such ways. If the sail doesn't have telltales, go by the simplest and oldest trimming rule of them all: ease the sail until it starts to luff, then sheet it in a bit until it stops luffing.

Sheeting angles

Why do some yachts have sheet tracks further outboard than others, and what effect does this have on sail trim? It depends on the type of yacht and what kind of headsail it carries. A performance

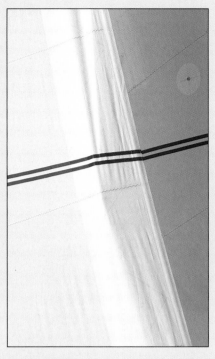

▲ If a spreader is trying to poke a hole in the genoa, you are overtrimmed and should ease the sheet a couple of inches.

cruiser with a fine entry to its hull can carry tighter sheeting angles than a displacement cruiser with a fuller entry, which needs a fuller shape in the headsail to keep it moving. A high-aspect ratio jib with little or no overlap can be sheeted further inboard than an overlapping genoa, which would otherwise backwind the mainsail and spoil the slot. If the sheeting angle is too wide, the slot will be too large with a corresponding loss of efficiency. If the sheet tracks are too far inboard, as the sail gets older and stretchier, the camber will move aft and get deeper, thereby increasing the exit angle

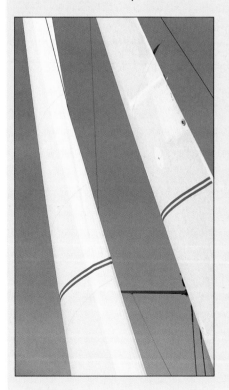

◄ You should aim to get the headsail and mainsail working in unison and trimmed so that the slot is the same all the way up. Ask the sailmaker to add camber stripes like these – they make the sail easier to read.

when the sail is sheeted in hard. It then becomes harder to get an ideal shape for pointing. Narrow sheeting angles are fine in flat water and low wind speeds but make it easy to oversheet the sail.

Generally, the higher the wind speed and the rougher the conditions, the further outboard the sheet leads should be, which is why most yachts designed for offshore cruising have wider sheeting angles than those intended primarily for inshore and coastal cruising.

The sheeting angle is the angle between the boat's centreline and a line drawn between the headsail's tack and its clew. To some extent this varies according to trim, but the position of the sheet track is fixed on cruising boats. A modern cruiser-racer will typically have a sheeting angle of between 10 and 13 degrees, while on a heavy, bluff-bowed cruiser, which needs power over pointing ability, it might be closer to 20 degrees.

Racing yachts often have two sets of sheet tracks; the inboard one is for pointing in flat water, the outer one for heavy-airs beating and for reaching.

The closest the typical cruising yacht can come to that degree of sophistication is to rig up a barber hauler, typically a length of line with a snap shackle or hook at one end. This is clipped to the genoa clew and led back to the cockpit through a snatchblock on the toe rail, set somewhat ahead of the forwardmost position of the genoa sheet car. It is most useful at or past a beam reach, when the genoa will not set properly unless the lead is moved forward and outboard. Another use for a barber hauler is to pull the clew inboard, allowing the boat to point higher in flat water.

Off the wind, the headsail's efficiency is greatly increased by moving the clew (A) outboard. The easiest way to do this is to rig a second sheet (B) running through a snatch-block on the toerail (D) while leaving the permanent sheet and its lead (C) in place. It takes less time than you think and pays dividends in boat speed.

How hard

A partly reefed genoa should never be sheeted in so hard that it is touching the shrouds or spreader – about six inches off is ideal. Because its belly will inevitably be fuller than that of a proper No. 2 genoa, trimming the sail in too hard will only result in more heeling and drag. A wider sheeting angle will keep the boat more upright and lessen the tendency of the mainsail to backwind.

The leech line

Most headsails have a leech line fitted to check flutter in the after edge of the sail. In light airs, a well-cut sail will usually remain stable, but as the wind increases there is a chance that the leech will start to flutter. You don't want this, for two reasons – it upsets the airflow across the sail, causing drag, and it will weaken the sailcloth. This is when a little adjustment of the leech line pays dividends. Too often, though, the leech line is tightened up when the flutter is actually caused by a poor sheet lead, so check the tell-tales first. If a sail doesn't need any leech line at all, there is a good chance that towards the top of its wind range the leech will be very hooked, while it may be fine in lower wind speeds.

▶ On boats with high-aspect non-overlapping headsails and sheet tracks set well inboard, like this Legend, it is even more important to rig an outboard sheet lead; otherwise, when sheets are eased, the sail twists off and loses drive.

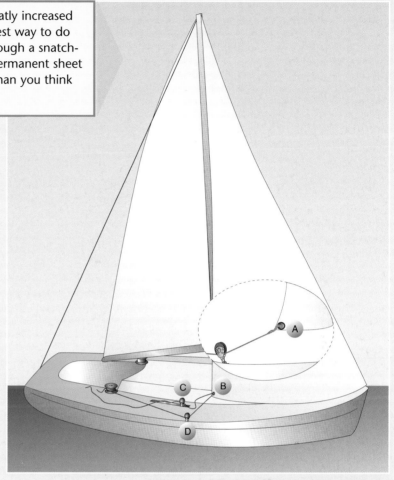

7 Mainsail Trim

Trimming tools

Windward trim

Mainsails can be infuriating to trim. Where luff tension and sheet lead position are the main variables in trimming your genoa, there are many more factors involved in achieving a perfectly-shaped mainsail.

▲ *The mainsheet and traveller are key trimming tools*

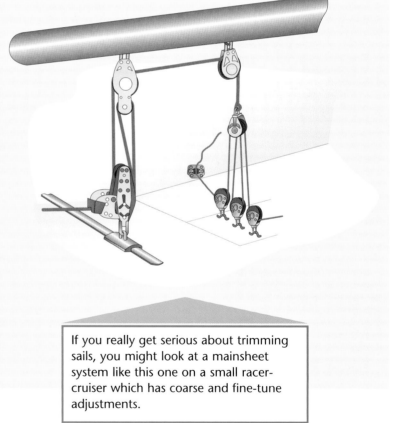

If you really get serious about trimming sails, you might look at a mainsheet system like this one on a small racer-cruiser which has coarse and fine-tune adjustments.

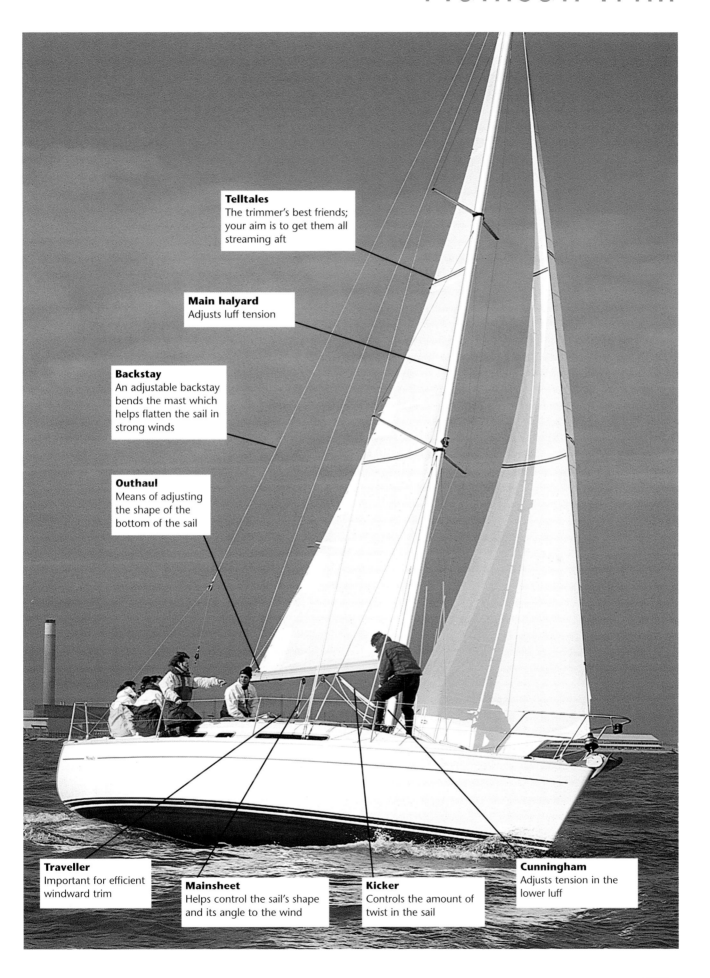

Telltales
The trimmer's best friends; your aim is to get them all streaming aft

Main halyard
Adjusts luff tension

Backstay
An adjustable backstay bends the mast which helps flatten the sail in strong winds

Outhaul
Means of adjusting the shape of the bottom of the sail

Traveller
Important for efficient windward trim

Mainsheet
Helps control the sail's shape and its angle to the wind

Kicker
Controls the amount of twist in the sail

Cunningham
Adjusts tension in the lower luff

Sailpower

Trimming tools

Mainsheet

The mainsheet pulls the sail's clew in towards the boat's centreline and once past a certain point, it also exerts a downward force. Going upwind, used in conjunction with the traveller, the mainsheet performs two interrelated functions; to place the sail at the most effective angle to the wind, and to control leech tension. When you are going to windward it is the leech that will tell you how well the sail is trimmed. As the mainsheet is tensioned, the clew is pulled downwards, thereby tightening the leech so that it starts to 'close' or hook to windward. In some situations, for instance when going to windward in light airs, this is desirable; but in stronger winds, a closed or hooked leech creates drag, slows the boat, and causes weather helm. When the sheet is eased, the leech 'opens' or falls off to leeward. Too open a leech results in twist and loss of power. Finding the happy medium between these two extremes is one of the secrets of good mainsail trim.

Kicking strap

The kicking strap (aka boom vang) is a vital tool when you're sailing on a reach or a run. Its job is to control twist in the sail by keeping a downward pull on the boom, which would otherwise lift as the mainsheet is eased. When this happens, the top part of the sail will start to luff and spill wind. If the mainsheet is hardened in to prevent this, the bottom part of the sail will be overtrimmed and will stall out, while the top half will be undertrimmed. Judicious use of the kicker will take care of this problem. Generally, the kicker is not used when the boat is sailing to windward, as the tensioned mainsheet will exert ample downward pressure on the boom.

Traveller

The mainsheet traveller lets you change the angle of the boom relative to the boat's centreline, without operating the mainsheet, so you can change the boom angle without altering the sail shape. Hard on the wind, if the boat is heeling too much and the sheet is eased to get her back on her feet, the boom rises and the top of the sail twists off to leeward. By letting the traveller down to leeward instead, the sail can be depowered while correct trim is maintained.

When sailing to windward in medium airs you would usually set the traveller on the centreline. Easing the traveller in a puff, instead of dumping the sheet, keeps the luff of the sail at the correct angle to the apparent wind, which comes aft in a gust. If the traveller is eased as you come on to a reach, it acts like a kicker and keeps the boom from rising.

Some boats don't have a traveller, with the mainsheet taken to an eye on the cockpit sole instead. In this case the kicker must be used on the wind as well as off the wind; tightening the kicker and easing the sheet to allow the sail to set at a wider angle to the wind will have a similar effect to easing the main down the traveller.

▲ *Poor sail balance: here the headsail is setting nicely but there is too much twist at the top of the mainsail; sheet in a little.*

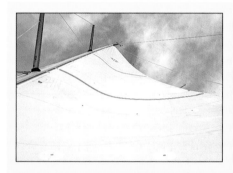

▲ *There is too much twist for the point of sail we are on – a close reach; more kicker tension to tighten the leech is called for.*

▲ *As the wind picks up, a little twist in the main is no bad thing. The traveller has been eased down the track to depower the sail, hence the backwinding.*

Halyard

The halyard has an important role to play in controlling the location of the draft in the sail. More halyard tension moves the draft forward in the sail and opens up the leech (desirable in stronger winds); less tension allows the draft to move aft and tightens the leech (desirable in light airs). For windward sailing, the sail's maximum draft should be about 40-45 per cent aft of the luff. If the halyard is too tight, you'll often see vertical creases near the luff. Ease it until they disappear. If there is not enough tension, you'll see horizontal wrinkles down the luff.

Cunningham

The halyard will always tension the upper part of the luff more than the lower part, because of friction in the luff groove or sail slides. The Cunningham provides the means of tensioning the lower part of the luff, using a small tackle hooked into an eye about six inches above the tack. Its effect is to flatten the lower part of the sail and move the draft forward. Don't write this off as a racer's toy; it's a shame that Cunninghams are rarely seen on cruising boats for they can be a useful tuning aid, especially on sails that are past their best.

MORE RULES OF THUMB

▲ *The wrinkles emanating from the clew indicate that the mainsheet or kicker is set up too hard; consequently there is too much mast bend for the conditions.*

No two cruising yachts are exactly alike and nor will their sails be trimmed in exactly the same way. There are some rules of thumb which, generally speaking, will apply to almost any bermudian-rigged yacht.

• In light airs, a fuller sail is needed. Ease backstay, halyard and sheets.

• Don't try to point too high in light airs – better to sail a little lower and make more speed.

• For pointing in flat water, you need a flatter headsail with a fine entry – leech just off the spreader, a straight forestay, halyard eased until draft is about 40 per cent back from the luff.

• In choppy conditions, increase backstay and halyard tension to keep the forestay tight and the draft forward in the sail. Easing the sheet a little will give the sail more drive. Do not try to point too high.

• Strong wind beating requires plenty of forestay tension, lots of halyard tension, sheet lead moved aft to open the leech, headsail sheeted in hard.

• Every time the forestay tension is adjusted, halyard tension needs to be checked.

• Bring sheet leads forward when bearing away to a reach.

You can fiddle with sail trim all day and still end up with a sorry-looking set to the headsail if the boat's rig is not properly set up and tuned. Nor will any amount of trimming make a tired old sail set well. If all else fails, enlist the aid of a sailmaker.

Sailpower

▲ *The mainsail is too flat for the conditions; the leech is closed so the top telltale has stalled.*

▶ *Beating into a fresh breeze, the mast is too straight, so the sail is too full; some backstay tension is needed.*

▶▶ *There's some mast bend evident here, but a little more backstay will flatten the sail and open the upper leech to spill wind.*

Outhaul

The clew outhaul affects the camber of the lower part of the sail. Tighten the outhaul and the lower section of the sail is flattened for windward work; ease it when you come off the wind and maximum depth is needed. The outhaul is used to best effect when combined with a loose-footed main or a shelf foot – an extra 'bag' of sailcloth built into the foot of the sail which gives it more fullness off the wind. When the outhaul is tensioned, the shelf foot is closed up.

Flattener

Some boats have a flattening reef instead of an adjustable clew outhaul. A line runs through a cringle set a foot or so above the clew, and is tensioned in the same way as a reef pennant, flattening the lower part of the sail and raising the end of the boom. On sails with flattening reefs, the clew is often shackled or lashed to the end of the boom.

Backstay

With an adjustable backstay the mainsail will be easier to trim in medium to heavy airs. Backstay tension bends the middle of the mast forward, flattening the sail. It also tensions the forestay (on a masthead-rigged boat).

▲ *The outhaul is used to tension the foot of the sail in medium to fresh breezes.*

LEECH TELLTALES

Telltales are almost as important for mainsail trim as they are for gauging headsail trim. I say 'almost' because many cruising boats don't have mainsail leech telltales and their owners seem to get by quite happily. But I like them because mainsails – especially fully-battened mainsails – can be a lot harder to read than genoas, and telltales help you judge mainsheet tension.

Leech telltales should be made from a tough nylon cloth, about eight inches long. Get your sailmaker to add them during the winter valet or fit them yourself. You can get by with three or four, sewn onto the batten ends. They work best when the apparent wind is eight knots or more. The top one tells you when the sail is oversheeted and the leech is too closed, by disappearing around to leeward. Ease the sheet to get some twist into the sail and it should fly straight aft.

If it streams aft for about half the time, in 10 knots or so of wind, then leech tension is about right. In heavier air all the telltales should stream straight aft. If the middle telltales break while the top one is streaming well, it indicates that the main is too full in the middle, and some halyard tension or mast bend is called for. If this does not help, the jib may be sheeted too closely, interfering with air flow along the mainsail; try easing it a little.

Telltales on the ends of the top three battens will help you to keep tabs on the how your mainsail is performing.

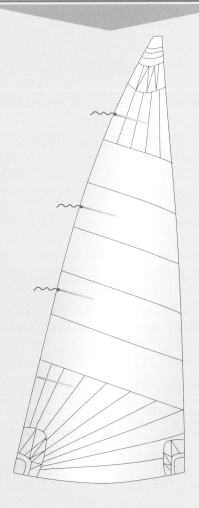

▷ *The top telltale has disappeared, indicating that the upper leech of the sail is too closed and the sheet should be eased. The main halyard has already been eased to flatten the sail entry so it backwinds less.*

Sailpower

Windward trim

Light airs

The sail needs to be full, particularly when sailing in choppy seas. In smooth water the sail can be a bit flatter, although it's best to err on the side of fullness. Ease the halyard tension until the draft is about 50 per cent aft of the luff. This is easier said than done – it can be difficult to tell where that dratted draft is, unless you have got your sailmaker to add camber stripes to the sail, although full battens will also indicate where the sail is deepest.

Ease the outhaul to increase the fullness in the lower part of the sail. The boom should be as close as possible to the boat's centreline, but never above it. If the boat has a traveller, pull it to windward of the centreline; this lets the sheet hold the boom in place without exerting too much of a downward pull on the leech, which should be slightly curved to weather. The tighter the leech, the higher the boat will point, though it will not necessarily perform better. Watch your telltales and boatspeed; in really light airs, don't try to point too high.

Medium airs

Increase halyard tension until horizontal wrinkles in the luff disappear and the draft moves forward. This will open the leech. Harden up on the outhaul a little to flatten the lower third of the sail. Set the traveller on the centreline and tighten the sheet until the telltales are flying correctly. If there is too much weather helm, gradually ease the traveller to leeward.

Heavy airs

Keep hardening up on the halyard and Cunningham to get the draft further forward. Tension the outhaul as much as possible, or take in the flattening reef. The sail should be very flat. Harden up the mainsheet. Keep easing the traveller down the track as the wind increases. If the boat is heeling too much, and as a last resort before reefing, ease the mainsheet a little until the sail is luffing and the top twists off to spill wind.

BALANCING MAINSAIL AND HEADSAIL

We have discussed the trimming of headsail and mainsail as if they are two separate identities. The basis of effective sail trim is to treat the sailplan as a single entity, adjusting the areas forward of, or abaft, the mast to achieve the elusive harmony known as balance.

You'll know when you've got there; the boat will be sailing fast, sails drawing well and telltales flying perfectly, the helm light. If the balance is all wrong, the tiller will be up around your ears, the wake will look like a tortured S, the boat will be heeling too far and the jib telltales will be drooping accusingly or flying around at random.

When sailing to windward, the golden rule is: trim the headsail before the mainsail. It reaches the wind first, and its trim has a significant effect on the main. Once the jib is set

▲ Bad trim: the main is oversheeted, the traveller is too far up the track, and the sail is too flat. The boat is stalled and making leeway.

correctly, with sheeting angle, luff tension and sheet tension just right, turn your attention to the mainsail. Trim the traveller and mainsheet as described above. If the helm is too heavy, ease the traveller down its track to widen the angle the boom makes with the boat's centreline. This will lighten the helm and decrease the boat's heel. Finding the right combination of mainsheet tension and traveller location is a matter of trial and error.

On boats with the headsail sheet tracks set close to the boat's centreline, the main may start to backwind as soon as it is eased down the traveller. The tendency then is to oversheet the mainsail until it stops luffing, but this does more harm than good; it will increase heel and weather helm. As long as the backwinding isn't excessive it won't affect the boat's speed or balance. In fact over-sheeting the mainsail is one of the most common mistakes made on any point of sail.

As the boat comes on to a reach, make sure that what is done to the mainsail is also done to the headsail; if you move the jib sheet lead forward to reduce twist, harden up the kicker to do the same to the mainsail, and so on. Having trimmed the sails, don't keep fiddling with them. Sit back and let the boat settle down. Wander up to the foredeck and look up at the slot between headsail and main. As long as the curves of the sails match, you won't be far wrong. Trimming sails isn't an exact science, and it needs plenty of experimentation.

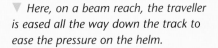
▼ *Here, on a beam reach, the traveller is eased all the way down the track to ease the pressure on the helm.*

▲ *A moderately backwinded mainsail won't affect the boat's performance, but over-sheeting will.*

▲ *This is more like it. The traveller has been let down the track a little and the sheet has been eased. The helm is lighter and there is less heel.*

8 Downwind Sailing

The most basic of all the downwind rigs – running wing-and-wing, or goosewinged.

Sailpower

Efficient downwind sailing is a little more complicated than going to windward. On a hard beat, once the sails are trimmed, the biggest question is whether she'd go better with a reef. Running before the wind, there are any number of permutations to think about. Goose-winged or poled-out headsail, cruising chute or spinnaker, broad reach or run – plus the ever-present possibility of an unintentional, skull-cracking gybe. Small wonder that downwind sailing, even though the boat is upright and the motion kinder, is by no means the safest or easiest point of sail.

Central to this is the feeling of false security engendered by the drop in the strength of the apparent wind. Going to windward, the wind speed over the deck equals the strength of the true wind plus the boat's speed. If the boat is making five knots into a true wind speed of 13 knots, the apparent wind speed will be about 18 knots – reefing time for many yachts. As the boat comes off the wind the apparent wind speed gradually falls until, when the wind is dead aft, its speed equals the true wind speed minus the boat's speed. If boat speed is six knots, the 13 knots of true wind will feel like 7 knots, barely enough to ruffle your hair, and you'll be thinking about getting some extra sail up.

Herein lies the root of most problems experienced when sailing down wind. It is all too easy to underestimate the wind's strength, and none too easy to keep tabs on a wind that is increasing. When it's time to come onto the wind again, the transition from easy run to rail-down beat always seems to be an unpleasant surprise. For the same reason, inexperienced crews are often unprepared for the shock that comes with the sail-flapping, rig-shaking violence of a broach.

Downwind sail trim

Coming off a good beat to windward onto a broad reach, it's tempting merely to ease the mainsheet out until the sail's just about on the spreaders and then enjoy the relaxing feel of a boat sailing free. To get the best out of the mainsail, though, you'll need to do a little work. The apparent wind speed will have dropped considerably, so the sail will want to be trimmed again. For starters, a vertical crease may have appeared near the luff, meaning there is too much luff tension. If you tensioned the backstay when beating to stop the headsail luff from sagging to leeward, and/or to induce some mast bend to flatten the mainsail, ease it off. If the vertical crease persists, ease the main halyard until it disappears, to be replaced by small horizontal wrinkles down the luff. The outhaul, if there is one, can be freed off to let the bottom of the sail assume a fuller shape. You want the sail to look quite baggy.

The top of the sail is likely to have too much twist in it, ie the top third will be sagging further to leeward than the rest, so the kicker will probably need to be hardened up until the top batten is parallel to the boom. (If the sail is fully battened, just go by the last couple of feet before the leech.) In very light airs, though, the weight of the boom alone may be enough to take the twist out.

Horizontal wrinkles in the luff of the headsail and mainsail (left) indicate that there is insufficient halyard tension for the wind strength. Vertical creases (right) mean that the halyard is over-tensioned.

Why is twist such a bad thing? Too much of it, especially in a strong breeze, can encourage the boat's tendency to roll downwind, making it harder to control. It lets more of the sail push and chafe against the leeward spreader and rigging. Also, it is inefficient, because a significant part of the sail is producing less thrust than the remainder.

Once the main is sorted out, you can think about the headsail. Downwind sailing is the one time a saggy headstay helps performance. It makes the genoa fuller and more powerful, and, as with the mainsail, easing the halyard until the luff starts to wrinkle will help even more. When the headsail sheet is eased, the top of the sail will twist off to leeward and lose its drive, so the sheet car will need to be moved forward to increase the downward pull on the clew. This only works up to a certain point, after which the bottom half of the sail will have too much curvature in it. You'll know when this happens because the three sets of luff telltales will all be doing different things. Now the sheet lead needs to be moved outboard for true efficiency. In an ideal world, you would rig a barber hauler by leading a spare sheet through a snatch block on the toerail and bending it on to the genoa clew. This opens up the slot between main and genoa and lets the sail 'breathe' more efficiently. Most cruising sailors just accept that the sail is not perfectly trimmed, and either ignore the telltales or sail by the middle set.

As you come further off the wind the genoa will be providing progressively less thrust as it is blanketed by the mainsail. Now the time has come to ponder the alternatives. There is something to be said for sailing high enough to keep the genoa full and drawing, and broad-reaching towards the destination in a series of gybes. Although more distance will be covered, the boat will usually sail faster on a broad reach than a run, and if the helmsmen are inexperienced there is much less chance of a crash gybe. However, it goes against the grain for many sailors to be heading away from a downwind destination.

In flat water and with the wind dead aft or thereabouts you can goosewing the genoa out to weather, but on boats with their headsail sheet tracks set well inboard this requires a lot of concentration on the helmsman's part because the headsail leech will always be curling to leeward and the sail needs little excuse to collapse. Barber-hauling the headsail is the only solution. In any case, if there is any sea running it doesn't take much to roll the wind out of the sail. If you're going to be on this point of sail for a while it's time to think about poling out the genoa.

Poling out the headsail

In light airs, a good old-fashioned whisker pole is the simplest and cheapest way of holding a headsail out to windward. It need be little more than a long, lightweight boathook or length of aluminium tubing or, if you can get it, bamboo, a little longer than the base of the foretriangle. Many whisker poles just have a spike at the business end which is pushed through the sail's clew ring, but the inboard end needs to be clipped to the mast ring. The sheet lead will probably need to be as far forward as practicable, at which point the sheet will probably chafe on the guardrail, so you may want to rig a barber hauler.

Whisker poles don't need topping lifts or downhauls because the clew of the sail can (usually) support their slight weight. On bigger boats, most of us will prefer to use a proper spinnaker pole to hold out the headsail and this will become essential in anything but light airs and flat seas. The genoa's

▲ Sailing wing-and-wing, with the headsail poled out and the mainsail secured with a preventer, is a safe, efficient way to run before the wind.

Here's a foolproof way of poling out your genoa for the long haul. Set up the pole with a topping lift (1), downhaul (2) and an afterguy (3). That way you'll be able to ease the sheet (4) without the pole swinging forward and crashing into the forestay. An even more foolproof method, which will let you trim in the genoa on either tack while leaving the pole and lines up, is to set it up as per the inset detail. Use a spare sheet (A) through the pole jaw while leaving the proper sheets (B) to hang free. If you need to come on to the wind or gybe, just cast off the spare sheet.

◀▲ *A set-up in which the headsail can be tacked or gybed without having to drop the pole. Topping lift, downhaul and afterguy hold the pole in position. An extra sheet (yellow) is led through the pole jaw and tied to the clew. Neither of the proper sheets go through the pole jaw.*

TELESCOPIC POLES

Note that a standard-size spinnaker pole has its limitations when it comes to poling out genoas with a large overlap. The pole will be too short to fully extend the sail to windward, and in heavy airs with a sea running, it would be prudent to take a few rolls in the genoa to flatten the poled-out sail. If you are using a telescopic pole, bear in mind that these are not strong enough when fully extended to take much punishment – when it starts to blow, you'll have to reef your pole along with your headsail.
If you're heading off on a tradewinds passage, and have room for it, you might consider making a longer 'light airs' pole – about 1.25 x J. This need not cost a fortune if you purchase the end fittings and the aluminium tubing separately.

clew tends to move around with the motion of the boat and the pole's topping lift and downhaul help to stabilise the sail and stop the wind from being shaken out of it. They also allow headsail twist to be controlled – just juggle topping lift/downhaul until the pole end is at the right height.

With the headsail sheet led through the pole jaw to its winch and trimmed in, we're all set up. But what happens if we need to come up onto the wind quickly, say to avoid a collision? As soon as the weather sheet is let go the sail will shoot off ahead of the forestay, bringing the pole with it. Now, for an exercise in real frustration, try dragging the genoa to the other side of the boat by pulling on the leeward sheet, with the pole hard against the forestay and the sail flogging for all it's worth. By the time the mess has been untangled, the reason for this sudden evasive action will have become much more compelling. (This scenario also illustrates why the pole jaw should never be clipped through the sail's clew cringle, or through the eye of the sheet bowline).

The addition of a guy, made fast to the outboard end of the pole and run back to the cockpit outside the guardrails, is an easy and foolproof way to avoid such an embarrassing, and potentially dangerous, fiasco. If the need arises to head up to weather quickly and get the genoa down to leeward, the guy will stop the pole from swinging forward and fouling things up while you gybe. Then the pole can be pulled against the shrouds and held in position. The guy will also stop the pole from damaging the headfoil extrusion.

For a true belt-and-braces approach, you could try rigging an extra sheet. This is a system I have used on several ocean passages and it works well.

Sailpower

The extra sheet goes through the jaws of the pole in place of the 'proper' sheet, and is taken to a cockpit winch via a snatch block on the toe rail. If you need to just gybe the genoa so you can go to windward, all you have to do is free the extra sheet and pull the headsail through the foretriangle in the normal fashion. If you need to gybe in a hurry so you can go to windward on the opposite tack, the extra sheet is freed and the 'proper' sheet is used to trim the headsail. In order to come onto a close reach you'll need to top the pole up as high as possible, pull it hard against the shrouds with the guy, and take a few rolls in the genoa. All this can be done in little longer time than it takes to read these paragraphs.

Such a rig is as foolproof a set-up as you can get, making it possible to come on to the wind on either tack without anyone having to go on to the foredeck to drop the pole. It's especially valuable for shorthanded crews. A little extra time spent rigging an afterguy, and possibly a second sheet, is a small penalty to pay for the peace of mind. A good argument for the second sheet – which can be any old length of low-stretch line – on long passages is that it saves your expensive genoa sheets from chafing in the pole jaws.

POLING OUT TIPS

- It is easier to roll the genoa away, rather than try to gybe it across.

- Set up the pole and adjust the uphaul, downhaul and guy until it is horizontal.

- Clip the sheet into the pole jaw. This is easier if the jaw is facing up. Do not clip the jaw through the leech cringle or the sheet bowline.

- Unroll the sail while winching in the sheet.

- Using the guy, pull the pole aft until it is almost touching the shrouds.

- Trim the sail until the sheet bowline is touching the pole jaw.

- Sight up the genoa. If there is too much twist – ie, the leech is fluttering at the top – adjust the pole downwards.

- A 140 or 150 per cent genoa will often need to be rolled up a couple of turns before it will set properly when poled out.

Trade wind rigs

The least complicated setup for extended downwind sailing is to go wing-and-wing, with the headsail poled out to windward and the mainsail out to leeward as far as it will go and securely strapped in place with preventers. Countless cruisers have crossed oceans under this rig, which is relatively quick to set up and is far more forgiving than running under spinnaker, but few would argue that it is ideal for trade wind sailing.

The biggest drawback of leaving the mainsail up for downwind work which can stretch into days or weeks is the long-distance sailor's arch-enemy, chafe. No matter how immovably you think you have trussed the boom, the sailcloth is constantly moving against the lower shrouds and the spreaders. The stitching starts to fray and, on fully-

PREVENTERS

The boom is a killer-in-waiting and the possibility of an accidental gybe should be at the forefront of every skipper's mind. Rigging a preventer will eliminate this ever-present danger. Preventers are also useful in reducing chafe and wear. When beam or broad reaching in light airs and a bit of a swell, the mainsail tends to roll with the boat and crash from side to side, with consequent wear and tear on the sail and the crew's nerves. Rig a line or tackle from the mid-boom to the toerail just forward of the shrouds, harden it up, and it'll act in opposition to the mainsheet to keep the boom in one place. The sail might still slat but you just have to live with that.

This situation shouldn't lead to an unwanted gybe, unless the helmsman is particularly dozy. A very broad reach or dead run in a blow is a different story, and it's then that you will want to rig a more serious preventer.

In anything more than light airs, the accepted method is to run the preventer line from the end of the boom all the way to a block near the bows and back to the cockpit. It's best to use a line that's light enough to break in the event of the boat broaching to leeward and being pinned down with the mainsail held aback by the preventer; the line will then be bearing hard against the shrouds with the full weight of sail and boom on it, and if something has to go, better the preventer than the rig. For the same reason, the preventer should be made fast to a winch or a cleat in the cockpit so that it can be released or cut instantly.

Many experienced offshore sailors use small-diameter nylon mooring warps for preventer lines because they will stretch more than polyester line, and are much more forgiving if the end of the boom dips into the sea when running hard. If the boat does broach or gybe, nylon line will let the boom travel much further than a polyester preventer and may still let the main partially gybe, while damping the speed at which it does so. If a mid-boom preventer is used in such heavy conditions there is a risk of bending or breaking the boom.

Another situation where a preventer is useful arises when you're sailing with a big following sea. The mainsail will sometimes backwind and invert as the boat accelerates down the face of a wave and exceeds the apparent wind speed; if this coincides with a roll to windward, or the helmsman steers too low, it's all too easy to gybe.

There are situations in which it's either foolish or impractical to rig a preventer, for instance when sailing in confined or crowded areas when swift evasive action may be needed, or when repeated gybes are called for and releading the preventer just becomes a nuisance. Those who sail in heavily-trafficked waters might think about patent gybe preventers like the Scott Boomlock or Dutchman boom brake; they slow down the speed at which the boom whistles across the cockpit, and can be left permanently rigged.

Rubber preventers are also available, and these are fine for putting the boom to sleep on a reach but shouldn't be trusted while running. I once saw a boat fitted with one of these gybe all-standing, and seconds later the preventer flicked the boom back across the cockpit like a giant elastic band just as the crew were picking themselves up off the cockpit sole.

While a preventer will let you sail by the lee with a certain degree of confidence, and will stop the

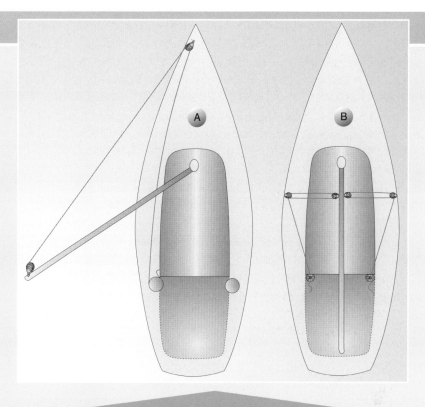

Here are two ways of rigging a gybe preventer: (A) is recommended for offshore sailing in big seas, where there is a chance of immersing the boom end in the water as the boat rolls. If the preventer was rigged further forward, the boom could break. The twin preventers rigged in method (B) work well for coastal cruising, and can also be used to ease the boom over during a gybe. Whichever way you rig a preventer, its tail must be brought back to the cockpit so it can be freed in a hurry.

boom from braining those in the cockpit while you get back on course, it should be treated in the same way as guardrails – as more of a psychological deterrent than a physical one. Sail as if it wasn't there, and you'll probably never need it. Good helming will reduce the need for a preventer, but a preventer won't reduce the need for good helming.

Double preventers

Those who sail short-handed need a foolproof, easily operated preventer system. An excellent way to achieve this is to set up a semi-permanent preventer on each side of the boom. Use 2:1 tackles, with the upper blocks attached to the midpoint of the boom and the

lower blocks shackled or clipped to the toerails by the mast. The preventer tails are then led back to cleats in the cockpit. In conjunction with the mainsheet, this set-up allows the boom to be locked in any position, and you can use it to control the speed of a gybe. Just winch in on the windward preventer line while the other is surged around a winch until the boom is on the centreline, then eased as the boom comes across the boat. Having these preventers rigged is a real boon when reaching in light-medium airs, when it lets you put the boom to sleep. In harbour, the lower blocks can be unclipped and the tackles stowed along the boom to keep the side decks clear.

Sailpower

battened sails, the cloth on the batten pockets will wear away in double-quick time. Sacrificial patches of sticky-backed dacron help, but Murphy's Law dictates that the day you can't be bothered dropping the sail to stick another one on is the day you end up with a hole in your batten pocket. A good tip for boats embarking on trade wind passages is to tape foam-rubber pipe insulation over the spreaders. It won't look elegant but it will save a lot of wear on the sail.

Fractionally-rigged boats (and the kind of modern masthead rigs which also have aft-swept spreaders) are prime candidates for chafe because the mainsail cannot be eased out very far before it bears on the spreaders and cap shrouds. No matter how hard you strap the boom down, you won't be able to ease it much past the ideal trim setting for a beam reach before the sail's rubbing merrily away on the hardware.

Chafe aside, you're always fretting about the long-term effect of such pressure against the shrouds and spreader roots; fluctuations in wind strength and boat speed mean that the weight of air in the sail is seldom constant and you can often see the spreader deflecting several inches in response to the changing loadings. When the wind falls light and there is a decent leftover swell, the main tends to backwind as the boat accelerates down the back of a wave and then fills with a bang as she slows to climb the next one, setting the entire rig twanging along with the crew's nerves. Full battens only make this worse because they invert and flick forward with greater velocity.

Nor does heavy weather give you any respite from worry. On a really lively run, a squared-off boom tends to dip into the water as the boat rolls and if the preventer has been set up hard – as it should be – the boom can easily bend or break.

If there is no likelihood of having to go to windward in the foreseeable future, it makes sense to rid of the mainsail altogether and let the front end do the work.

Twin headsails

In the days before windvane steering gears, it became standard practice for cruisers faced with long downwind passages to drop the main and instead pole out a pair of specially-made matching headsails opposite each other. By taking the sheets back to the tiller via blocks on the quarters, the boat could be made to steer itself. As it veered to windward and the apparent wind speed increased, so did the thrust on the windward sail. The load would be transferred to the sheet, which would pull the tiller to windward and make the boat turn back downwind. And vice-versa. As the pressure on the sails equalised the tiller would centre itself.

The earliest recorded use of this set-up was in the 1930s and it was eagerly adopted by, among many others, Eric Hiscock, who recounts in *Wandering Under Sail* the process of setting up 'twin spinnakers' on *Wanderer II*. As a basic, reliable, easily managed long-distance downwind sailplan it is just as valid today as it was 70 years ago. Without the mainsail, the sailplan's centre of effort is so far forward that it pulls the boat instead of pushing it, eliminating the imbalance that comes with having two sails of unequal area set one in front of the other and

---

THE TRADITIONAL WAY

Peter Keig has circumnavigated twice, single-handed, in his self-built steel Roberts 38. This is his favoured downwind rig.

'After many miles and much experimentation I have found twin headsails by far the best and safest system. My twin headsail rig requires a second forestay to carry the extra sail. The secondary forestay, made of a lighter 1x19 wire than the headstay, is attached via a toggle to the masthead and there is a 4:1 purchase on the lower end, snap-shackled to the bow. When not in use the stay is detached, moved aft, and shackled to a ring bolt in the deck close to the mast. This system, as opposed to side-by-side twin forestays, retains the tension in the main forestay for windward sailing.'

'The two spinnaker poles, mounted in a double car on the mast track, are held captive by a topping lift, a foreguy to the bow and an aft guy to the stern. They are positioned horizontally and 6ft 6in off the deck to prevent head injuries when walking forward. The headsail sheets are reeved through single blocks on the outboard ends of the poles, lessening the possibility of chafe as the poles work back and forth, and led aft to the cockpit winches via blocks on the transom.'

'The hanked-on second headsail is easy to hoist and to douse it, just let go the halyard and it bunches up between the bow and pole end. Slacken off the sheet and the sail can be pulled inboard and on to the deck. Should the wind increase, the boat will soon be running with only one headsail and as that is reefed, the pole decreases in usefulness and is eventually stowed.'

An alternative running rig – genoa poled out to windward and a second headsail set flying and sheeted through a block on the end of the main boom.

Sailpower

working in opposite planes. Vane gears are not at their best downwind when the apparent wind is light and the natural balance of the twin-headsail rig helps them do their job. It also lessens the workload, and therefore the current draw, of electronic autopilots.

Over the years, the restless minds of many yachtsmen have turned to developing and refining the 'twins'. The sails evolved into high-clewed 'yankee' types, to keep the pole ends well clear of the water as the boat rolls and coincidentally giving good forward visibility. High-clewed sails are also more likely to keep drawing strongly in big seas where low-clewed sails can lose the wind in the troughs.

Traditionally, each sail was hanked to its own forestay, which meant that many long-distance cruisers had to add a second headstay as well as an extra halyard and topping lifts and downhauls for two poles. Later experiments saw the two sails stitched together along the luff and either hanked to a single forestay or set on a furling gear. This in turn led to the development of the *bollejan*, as the Dutch called it, a two-ply genoa which could be peeled apart for downwind running and, with the two plies together, used to reach or beat to windward. It enjoyed much favour with singlehanded ocean racers for a time before the advent of reliable furling gears.

Although seldom used for windward work these days – it is not as efficient as a 'proper' jib – derivatives of the *bollejan* are used as running sails on many cruising boats, because they will fit into a single-groove headfoil. Shortening and making sail in response to the often fluky trade winds, which can go from force 2 to force 8 and back again in a matter of hours, is as easy as rolling away a genoa.

Of course, there is no real need to have headsails made specially, and nor do they need to be identical in shape or area. Two headsails can be set on a twin-groove headfoil, but don't use a second genoa halyard or spinnaker halyard to hoist the second sail because it will wind around the headfoil if you try to roll the sails away. The easiest way to get around this problem is to shackle a block to the lower part of the furling gear's top swivel, with a mousing line led down to the drum. When required, a halyard is fed through the block with the mousing line used for the second headsail. When it's time to come on to the wind again, after the sail is handed and the halyard is removed, the block and mousing line can be left in place and will roll up with the genoa.

Nor is a second pole essential, if you sheet the leeward sail through a snatchblock on the end of the squared-off main boom. The sail can even be set flying, though getting it down in a fresh breeze will provide an interesting diversion.

Cruising chutes and gennakers can also work well when sheeted through the end of the boom, as long as you have a spare sheet led forward of the boom to pull the sail inboard when it's being handed. If you are using an asymmetrical spinnaker in this way, it pays to put a reef in the main so that more unobstructed air can reach the head of the kite. You could then pole the genoa out to windward.

Dedicated downwind sails are nice to have, but if the budget won't stretch, you can make do with a couple of beaten-up old boat jumble genoas. They'll save wear and tear on your good sails and get you there just as quickly.

TWISTLE RIG

The twistle rig was invented by a British yachtsman in the early 1960s and used on a circumnavigation. Some thirty years later sailmaker Andy Cassell, of Ratsey and Lapthorn, resurrected the concept for the first Tradewind rally.

It is an ingenious twist on the twin pole, twin headsail method. The poles are secured to the sails but not the mast. The outboard ends are not clipped through the sail's clew rings. Instead, two short pendants bent to the clews are threaded through the pole jaws, down along the length of the poles, and cleated off. The poles' inboard ends are clipped to a stainless steel fabrication which acts as a universal joint, letting the poles move freely in the vertical and horizontal planes. The topping lift and downhauls are secured to this joint.

The sail is hoisted up the furler's luff groove and rolled away before the poles are attached. Then the poles are topped up and the sail unrolled. Once the poles are set up correctly, effectively suspended in mid-air, the twistle rig is trimmed with the sheets as in a convention-ally poled-out headsail. This all sounds a much more complicated than it is, as we found when we gave the twistle rig a trial run in the Solent. Certainly, it is less labour-intensive than setting up two conventional spinaker poles. The point of it all is to let the sails move about as the boat rolls so the poles don't transmit sail-induced heeling forces to the mast. In theory, it will dampen the rhythmic rolling expe-rienced by so many boats.

The twistle rig can be trimmed for a broad reach by easing the windward sheet out and hardening up the leeward one, but with the bonus that there are no guys to adjust. The only lines you touch are the sheets. It is quite forgiving – we had brought the boat slightly above a beam reach before the windward sail collapsed.

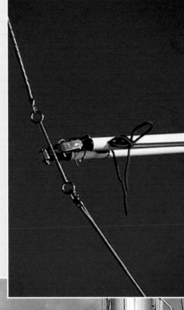

◄◄▼ The Twistle rig in action – these sails belong to a smaller boat. This ingenious rig with its 'floating' poles takes some of the strain out of downwind sailing. Twin headsails are attached to the poles, which in turn are suspended between the topping lift and the downhaul (inset).

Coloured sails

The spinnaker makes a powerful trade wind sail, as long as you have a good-sized crew who enjoy sailing the boat hard. The trades, especially in the Pacific, never blow constantly from one direction; the wind is always shifting around and varying in strength and this calls either for frequent trimming, a helmsman adept at steering to the spinnaker, or both. When things go wrong with a spinnaker, they often go wrong in a big way, especially when the 10 knots of wind over the transom builds to 15 or 20.

Most cruising couples wouldn't dream of setting the kite unless the seas are flat and the wind gentle, and who can blame them? Running dead downwind in a seaway, the boat's desire to roll will be encouraged

73

by the yawing of the spinnaker and broaching is an ever-present danger; sailing by the lee invites the mainsail to be taken aback, annoying even with preventers rigged, wandering too far to windward will see the sail collapse and then fill with a bang as you bear away again, shaking the boat right down to the keelbolts. This is not relaxing.

An asymmetric cruising chute will generally not set with the apparent wind angle less than around 140 degrees, so it doesn't make a good running sail unless it is poled out. If the tack is poled out like a symmetrical spinnaker, then you have the same problems of trim and steering surface; fine for short passages, but ultimately tiring for a small crew on a long voyage. The alternative is to pole the clew out to windward and run goosewinged, with the main to leeward. This is a forgiving and highly effective set-up for light conditions, but it requires an overlength or telescopic pole. When it's extended, a telescopic pole is nowhere near as strong as a regular spinnaker pole, and if it's used in a messy seaway it will bend at the slightest excuse.

Some cruisers have made over-length poles purely to help them wing out cruising chutes and genoas more efficiently. When an overlapping genoa is poled out, its shape is quite full. Plenty of camber in the sail is fine for light-airs running, but as the wind and seas build, a baggy sail will exaggerate the metronomic rolling motion cursed by so many who sail the trades. With a normal-length spinnaker pole you'll have to take a few rolls in the genoa to get it to set flat and tight and this takes away some useful sail area and often means you have to reef the main to balance the boat. A pole of about one and a quarter times J, the foretriangle base length, lets you use all of the sail in moderate airs when a tight, flat sail is desirable. It should ideally be longer, 140 per cent or so, for a cruising chute. Of course, that raises another problem – stowing such a long pole when it's not in use. Such is life.

The squaresail

What could be more efficient for trade wind sailing than a squaresail? Ewen Southby-Tailyour spend a good part of his childhood on a pilot cutter equipped with one such, and he had such fond memories of it that he had one made for his gaff-rigged Tradewind 35, *Black Velvet*.

With an area of nearly 800 square feet, *Black Velvet*'s squaresail provides a lot of drive in light to moderate running conditions. The 26ft yard is hoisted on a stay running from deck just before the mast to just above the crosstrees. It has two topping lifts so the yard's angle can be controlled and two braces which clip onto the end of the yard, as well as two sheets, so there is a lot of rope about.

It can be hoisted by one person 'at a pinch' but the job is easier with two. Once set, the sail can be brailed up from the deck, and it has a single row of reef points about a third of the way down – though the yard has to come down on deck to be reefed. It is at its best dead downwind, because the shrouds limit the extent to which the yard can be angled aft.

9 Spinnakers for Cruisers

Sailpower

The cruising sailor's relationship with the spinnaker is like the lion-tamer's with his cat. He can bend it to his will but never knows when it will turn on him; he can never relax. Perhaps this is why someone once described the process of dropping a spinnaker in a blow as like grabbing an angry tiger by the tail and trying to stuff it into a bag. This inbuilt mistrust and fear does the spinnaker scant justice. Used in the right conditions, and treated with respect, it's a terrific sail that can turn a slow, boring downwind run into an exciting, enjoyable experience.

Construction

Spinnaker design has evolved into three basic types: *cross-cut*, *radial head*, and *tri-radial*. There are still plenty of older cross-cut spinnakers around, but hardly anyone now makes them for bigger boats. They are full in the head and tend to stretch in the upper panels in a fresh breeze, so while they are fine on a run, reaching presented some problems. The radial head spinnaker has vertical panels at the top while the lower section is cross-cut. This cloth orientation reduces stretch at the head in heavy airs. Next came the tri-radial and star-cut, whose panels are orientated in the main directions of load and so are more resistant to stretching. Most sailmakers have their own 'brand' names for these cuts, and offer their own variations in panel layout and design. Some spinnakers are optimised for reaching and can be used as close as 50 degrees to the apparent wind, others are cut fuller for running.

It's important to tell the sailmaker whether the sail is to be used for cruising or racing, or a combination, as this will influence the type of cloth as well as the cut. There are many different kinds of spinnaker nylon; for a racing sail, a resin-filled, non-porous cloth which holds its shape well will be preferred, but this will not have the tear strength of a stretchier, more porous material which is better suited to cruising.

As far as cloth weights go, ¾oz is suitable for cruising boats up to 35ft, 1oz up to 45ft, and 1½oz will suit boats to 80ft.

Running gear

Boats of less than around 30ft LOA can get away with just three lines controlling the spinnaker – the halyard, sheet and guy. The sheet trims the sail, the guy holds the tack against the spinnaker pole, and once the sail is gybed, the sheet becomes the guy and vice versa. On bigger boats, and in heavier airs, the muscles of a weightlifter would be required to physically haul the sheet in to clip the pole end to it, so the control lines are doubled up to put a sheet and guy on each side of the boat. On the windward side, the guy will hold the clew against the pole, while the sheet is not doing any work, and on the leeward side the sheet will trim the sail while the guy hangs about doing nothing – hence the terms 'lazy' sheet or guy.

The other lines which you'll need to rig for spinnaker work are the topping lift and foreguy, or downhaul, which should run through a block located near the bows so it pulls the pole forward as well as down.

Three popular types of spinnaker: radial head (1), tri-radial (2) and star-cut (3). The latter two are generally better at reaching.

Once you have learnt its tricks, the spinnaker is a truly satisfying and very efficient sail.

Sailpower

Launch and recovery

Most spinnaker dramas happen when the sail is being set or doused. As long as some basic rules are remembered, there should be few problems.

• Make sure the halyard is on the correct side of the forestay. Place the bag about halfway between the mast and bow. All the spinnaker control lines – sheet, guy, halyard, topping lift and downhaul – must be rigged so that they will not become entangled with guardrails, shrouds, or spreaders, and it is always worth double-checking that there is no chance of a foul-up.

• You should always hoist or drop the spinnaker in the lee of another sail. To hoist, come onto a broad reach and whip the kite up in the wind shadow of the mainsail or (when reaching) the genoa. Speed is important when you're hoisting a kite so it's best done hand-over-hand from a standing position by the mast, but this can be dangerous unless someone else is tailing the sheet on a winch or pulling it through a clutch.

• When the kite is fully hoisted, pull the pole back to the desired position and only then trim the sheet. The sail should fill from the bottom upwards.

• To drop the sail, reverse the procedure. On a broad reach, ease the pole forward until it's on the forestay and let the guy out a few more feet while the helmsman steers downwind until the sail is blanketed by the main. Make the lazy guy fast to a cleat or coachroof grabrail (this will ensure the sail doesn't get away from you) then pull on the sheet and the sail should collapse. The sail can then be pulled down onto the foredeck or under the boom. Steadiness on the helm is important, as luffing up at the wrong moment could make the sail fill just when you don't want it to.

▲ *Always try to drop the spinnaker in the wind shadow of the mainsail.*

Flying the kite

Exact spinnaker trim is pretty difficult to describe. There are so many variables – wind strength, sea state, boat size, the cut of the sail – that it is only possible to generalise. There are some rules of thumb, though, that pretty well apply across the board, and these are quite basic.

• First, the sheet and guy leads need to be set up. Sheet leads should be about a spinnaker pole's length abaft the mast, which will put them near the quarter on most boats. In some situations the sheet leads will need to be moved forward, which is usually accomplished by means of barber haulers – a snatchblock on a line running from the cockpit through another block on the toe rail just abaft the shrouds. This is clipped to the spinnaker sheet and can be eased or tensioned to change the lead.

• The guy should be run through a block on the toerail at the point of maximum beam, which is usually halfway between mast and stern, and taken to the genoa sheet winch. Make sure the block is strong, because the guy is the most heavily loaded spinnaker control line.

• For broad reaching and running the pole should generally be kept at right angles to the apparent wind, though in light airs it can be trimmed a little further aft, and in heavy airs a few degrees further forward.

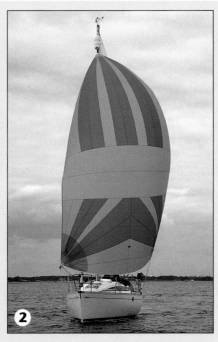

Trim tips

1 *The idea is to keep the clews level, so the pole needs to be lowered.*
2 *If the pole is too low, the sail won't set efficiently.*
3 *When the luff just starts to curl inwards, trim the sheet.*
4 *On a reach, an open leech will spill wind and lessen heeling*
5 *On a run, the pole is squared to bring the kite into clear air.*

• When reaching, as the apparent wind comes forward of about 120 degrees, trim the pole further forwards.

• Windward and leeward clews should be level. To achieve this, raise or lower the pole's inboard end on the mast track, keeping the pole perpendicular to the mast. Having it cocked up or down is bad practice because it brings the sail closer to the disturbed airflow from the mainsail.

• The pole's height will vary according to the wind strength – the aim is to keep the sail flying as high as possible, while keeping the clews level. In lighter airs the weight of the sheet will pull the clew down and the pole will need to be lowered.

• As the wind increases, lower the pole and bring the sheet lead forward to prevent the spinnaker from oscillating.

Sailpower

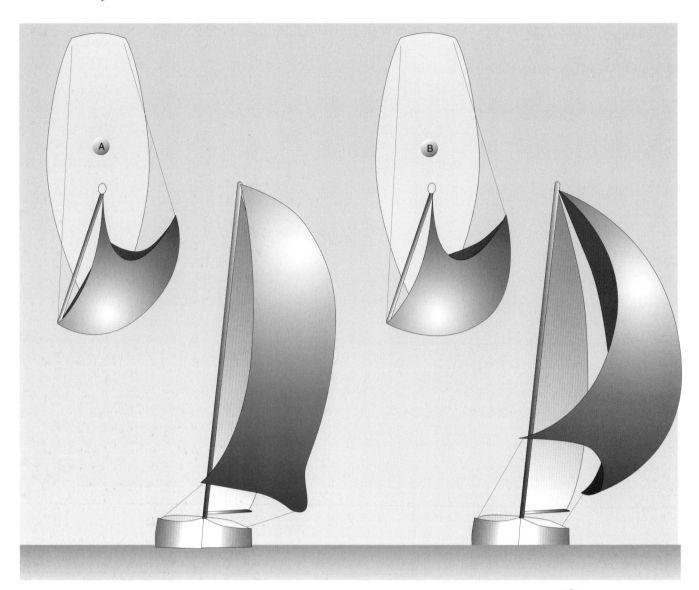

• If most of the luff curls inward (breaks) at the same time, the pole height will be about right. If the top third breaks first, raise the pole. If the middle third breaks first, lower the pole a little.

• On a reach, the leeward clew will tend to fly higher than the windward clew. The sheet lead needs to be moved aft when reaching, to let the leech open further away from the mainsail.

• With the wind close to the beam, it's desirable to get maximum draught in the sail as far forward as possible to prevent broaching. This can be achieved by lowering the pole.

• To trim the spinnaker, ease the sheet until the luff just breaks, then trim it in until it stops. On a broad reach or run, the sheet trimmer will do this, but on a reach, with the sheet strapped in tight, it will be up to the helmsman to steer to the spinnaker.

• Avoid a dead run whenever possible. It is faster to head up on to a broad reach; safer, too.

With the wind close to the beam, it is best to get the draught forward in the sail by lowering the pole (A). If the pole is too high (B), the sail will be too full and could overpower the boat.

Elements of trim: if the top third of the luff breaks first (1), the pole may be too low. If most of the luff breaks at the same time (2), the pole is about right. If the middle third breaks first, try lowering the pole a little (3).

Gybing the spinnaker

On smaller boats with single sheets and guys, the pole is end-for-ended during a gybe. Doubling up the lines to put a sheet and guy on each side makes it possible to gybe by lowering the pole until it clears the forestay, then lifting it on the other side of the boat – the dip-pole gybe.

If the boat has a babystay or inner forestay then it will almost certainly have twin poles, which makes the operation even easier; the second pole is set up to leeward, with the lazy guy is clipped to it, before the boat is gybed and the original guy let go.

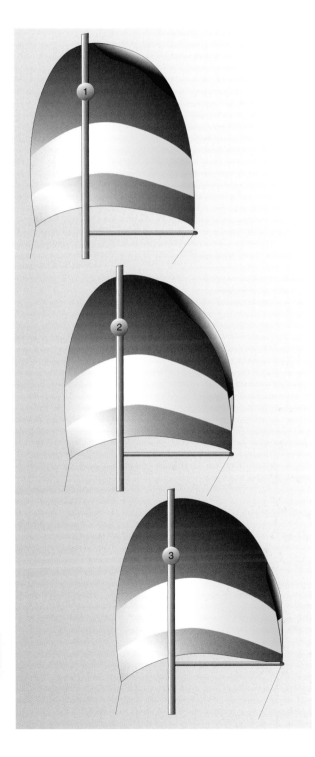

When broad-reaching or running, the pole should be kept at a right angle to the apparent wind (top); reaching, the pole will have to be taken closer to the wind in order to flatten the sail.

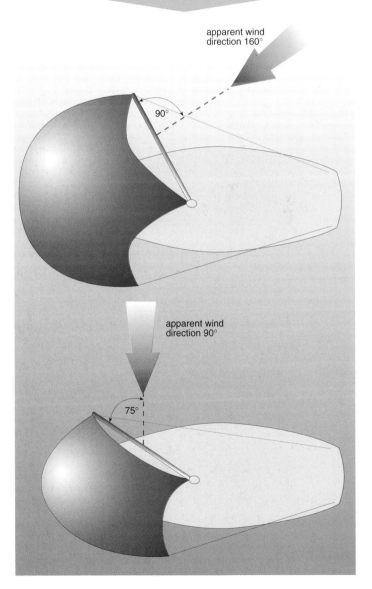

apparent wind direction 160°

90°

apparent wind direction 90°

75°

Sailpower

The basic dip-pole gybe: 1) Bear away on to a run. 2) Unclip the guy from the pole. 3) Keep the mainsail and spinnaker centred while the new guy is clipped into the pole end. 4) Gybe the main and pull the pole aft. 5) Trim the spinnaker.

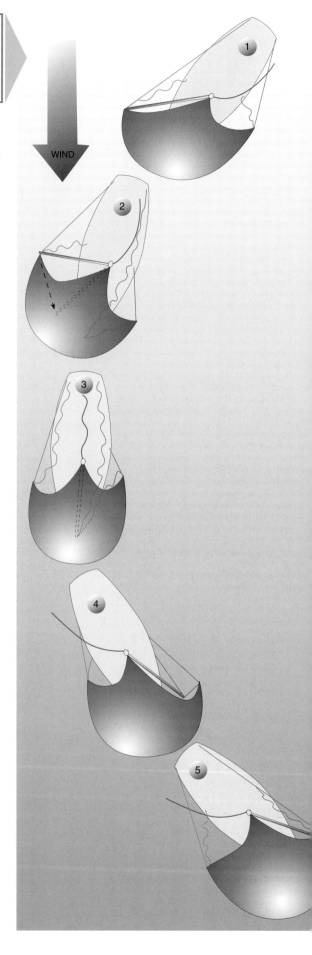

To let the pole drop away from the guy, it should always be rigged so that the jaws are facing upwards. The lazy sheet should always be kept over the top of the pole end; if it drops underneath it will trap the pole, stopping it from being lowered and swung inboard for a dip pole gybe. It is also important to let the best helmsman steer the boat. A spinnaker gybe is no time to have a novice on the helm. It calls for a fair amount of co-ordination and the ability to steer a straight course without being distracted by the goings-on on the foredeck. The basic procedures for these gybes are:

End-for-end gybe

- Bear away to a dead run.
- Trim the pole until the middle of the sail is on the boat's centreline .
- Unclip the pole from the mast and attach it to the leeward sheet.
- Release the other end from the windward sheet (guy) and clip it to the mast (in a breeze, it is wise to unclip the pole from the windward sheet before attaching it to the leeward one).

Dip-pole gybe

- Bear away to a dead run.
- Trim the pole until the sail is on the centreline.
- Free the guy and ease the topping lift so the pole drops down to the foredeck. If the trimmer and helmsman are working together, the sail can fly free while the gybe is being made.
- Take a bight of the lazy guy forward and clip it to the pole.
- Haul in on the new (ex-lazy) guy so the pole swings onto the other side of the boat.
- Take up on the topping lift.
- Winch the guy aft until the sail's clew is pulled to the pole end.

It's best to gybe the main at the same time as the spinnaker. If it's gybed sooner then it can blanket the spinnaker and make it collapse. In light airs you could sheet the main hard amidships and complete the gybe after the spinnaker has been gybed. Don't complete the gybe until everyone is ready. After the gybe, head up slowly on to the new course and trim the spinnaker.

FOUL-UPS

The sight of a spinnaker hour-glassed around a forestay, two huge bulges of cloth drawing merrily while the crew scurry around cursing, never fails to raise a smile – as long as it is happening to someone else. It's not quite so funny if you are one of the people staring up at the mess wondering what to do next.

It is the possibility of a foul-up that puts many cruisers off the thought of flying a spinnaker at all. In fact it's more of a certainty than a possibility – anyone who uses a spinnaker often enough will sooner or later have to deal with a wrap. More often than not, it will happen when the kite is being set. A twist may have been put into it when it was last packed, or a sudden roll when it's being hoisted will make the leech and the luff change places, or someone won't be quick enough with the sheet, or maybe it's just not your day. There it is – the dreaded hourglass.

The worst thing you can do is to head up to windward, or pull the pole back to try to fill the spinnaker in the belief that the air pressure will unwind the wrap. It will usually just tighten it. The best thing to do is to steer downwind to keep the wrap in the wind shadow of the mainsail so that the wind can't fill part of the spinnaker and tighten the wrap even more. If the sail is merely twisted around itself, some gentle tugging on the sheet and guy is often enough to untangle it. You could also try easing the halyard a little to make sure the swivel at the top of the sail is stuck in the block. If that doesn't work, get the sail down and repack it.

The really nasty hourglass is the one where the sail takes a turn around the forestay and then fills, tightening the cloth around the stay. If you tug on the foot or the leeches to try to get the kite to slide down the stay, the thin nylon will merely twist itself harder together. The first thing you should do is gybe the boat – the reversed airflow from the main will urge the spinnaker to rotate in the opposite direction so it unwraps itself from the stay. This method works nine times out of ten. If it doesn't, it's time to get the bosun's chair out – or reach for the knife.

Another thing that gives cruisers a certain malicious satisfaction is the not uncommon sight of a racing yacht's spinnaker streaming from the masthead like some giant banner, sheets and guys flailing. This is usually the end product of a broach, when the crew has freed off everything bar the halyard to get the weight out of the sail and the boat back on its feet. There are a couple of ways of coping with this. The most common is to come on to a dead run, and when the spinnaker starts to float downwards in the lee of the mainsail, grab the closest sheet or guy and ease the sail down. Another is to pull on either sheet or guy until a clew is within reach and then ease the halyard slowly, taking care that the spinnaker doesn't fill; in a breeze it can pull the boat over on her beam ends. In some cases there's no alternative but to let the halyard go and hope you can get to the sail before it sinks.

If the halyard breaks or chafes through or the swivel breaks, the sail will, if fortune smiles, float down beside the boat on the weather side and hang from the pole end. Turning away from the sail will bring it close enough to reach from the boat. Of course, the sail may just drop ahead of the boat and go underneath it, in which case you are in for a fun-filled time and, usually, a sizeable repair bill.

There are ways of guarding against hourglasses. Spinnaker nets are triangular contraptions of light line – like a skeleton jib hoisted between the headstay and mast to prevent the kite from being blown through the foretriangle and becoming fouled. There are lots of variations on the theme and it is not difficult to make one up. A spare genoa or spinnaker halyard will be needed to hoist it, though, and many modern boats don't have these.

▶ *The dreaded wrap – but it needn't ruin your day*

Sailpower

The dreaded broach

Sooner or later, every boat which flies a spinnaker will broach. Broaching is essentially a build-up of weather helm to the point where it overpowers every other influence. If the boat is sailed dead upright in flat water, with the spinnaker and main perfectly balanced, it will never broach.

Unfortunately such a combination of blessed circumstances is rare indeed. What all too often happens is that the boat is running hard in a bit of a seaway and the kite starts to oscillate, or a gust catches the helmsman unawares, or a quartering sea makes the boat heel quickly. Then the forces from both the spinnaker and the main will be concentrated on one side of the boat, making her heel further, and then she will want to come up into the wind. Given enough heel the rudder becomes ineffective, loses its grip, and the boat gripes violently and unstoppably to windward.

If your luck is really out of town, you will recover from the windward broach, have a nanosecond to congratulate yourself on your superior helmsmanship, and then the boat will roll the other way and broach to leeward instead. This is the really nasty one, with the mainsail either gybing viciously or, if held aback by a preventer, pinning the boat down. Plenty of boats have filled and sunk this way.

There is an easy way to avoid broaching with a spinnaker up. Only use one in light airs. According to the experts, 90 per cent of broaches are due to oversteering. The helmsman feels the load coming on to the rig and bears away just a bit too much, over-corrects, and whoopsie…

Spinnaker novices would be well advised to practice in light airs, flat, open water, and far away from an audience. The best way to learn how to fly a spinnaker is to go racing (preferably on someone else's boat). Racers keep their spinnakers up in conditions which would have most sensible cruisers well reefed down, so there's no better schooling. When you've broached half a dozen times on a lively run, using a spinnaker for more sedate cruising will hold few fears.

Asymmetric spinnakers

The humble cruising chute has come a long way. Not all that long ago they were regarded with contempt by the racing fraternity; now, rebadged as asymmetric spinnakers, they're the hot item with the go-fast crowd. It's nice to think that in an age where cruising yacht and sail evolution has been so profoundly influenced by racing rules, a sail developed purely for cruising has such a profound effect on racing. From small sports boats to Volvo Ocean Race yachts and America's Cuppers, asymmetrics have popped up everywhere.

Originally, the cruising chute was little more than a regular spinnaker with a triangular bottom panel to make its luff longer than its leech, allowing it to be flown without a pole, tacked down to the boat's stemhead. Over the last decade, since the racers became involved, design has come a long way. Asymmetrics can be cut flat for reaching or full for broad reaching; some of them will let you sail as close as 40 degrees to the apparent wind. They are wonderfully versatile sails.

PACKING THE SPINNAKER

Whether you use a snuffer or hoist from the bag, proper packing is essential for both kinds of spinnaker. To pack a spinnaker in a bag, start at the foot. Keep the clews separate, one on each side of the bag, and run your hands along the luff tapes, stopping every so often to stuff the body of the sail into the bag. Leave the clews and the head sticking out of the bag, with the head in the middle, and tie them apart so they can't twist around each other.

The easiest way to pack a chute into a snuffer is to do it on dry land. Make the head of the snuffer fast, attach the head of the spinnaker to it, then stretch out the spinnaker and make sure the edges are not twisted. Keeping some tension on the clews, pull the sleeve down over the sail.

You could also do this on board on a calm day, by attaching spinnaker head and sleeve to the halyard and hoisting the spinnaker slowly while pulling the sleeve down over the sail, keeping the edges separate.

◀ *A sleeve around the forestay will keep the tack close inboard and make the asymmetric easier to trim.*

The asymmetrical cut lends itself to a better airfoil shape than can ever be achieved with a symmetrical spinnaker, so it can be used closer to the wind. The shape gives more lift, and also cuts drag, and the flatter cut and open leech makes it less likely that the sail will overpower the boat.

The typical cruising chute will have a tri-radial cut and be made from reasonably heavy cloth, usually 1.5 ounce, because of the greater loads sustained when reaching.

Setting the asymmetric

The main attraction of asymmetrics is, of course, that they don't require a pole. Setting is easier than with a symmetrical kite. The sail's tack is made fast forward of the headstay with a long tack line, which should ideally be led via a block back to the cockpit, although it can be made off at a bow cleat. The sheet lead needs to be as far outboard and aft as possible; a block near the quarter is the best bet. Bringing the lead this far aft opens the leech of the sail to reduce heeling moment.

The sail is best hoisted in the lee of the main, as with a symmetrical spinnaker. Get it up as quickly as you can and don't tension the sheet until the sail is all the way up. To drop the sail, bear away until it is blanketed by the main, tie the sheet off, and ease the halyard quickly while pulling the sail down under the boom. Pull down on the leech hand-over-hand until most of the sail is down, then gather in the foot.

Trimming

Trimming an asymmetric is very easy compared to a symmetrical spinnaker, because there is no pole to worry about. The sail is sheeted through a block on or near the quarter and the tack needs to be located on a strong point forward of the forestay; a block on the bow roller is ideal. Preferably, the tack line should be long enough to run aft to the cockpit.

To make that the sheet lead is correct, go sailing in a light breeze. The tack line should be adjusted so that the tack is level with the top of the pulpit, with the halyard tightened sufficiently to take some of the curve out of the luff.

Head up to around 60 degrees apparent wind angle with the sail sheeted in hard, then slowly ease the sheet until the luff starts to curl. If it breaks in the top third of the luff, the sheet lead needs to move forward. If the luff breaks in its bottom half, the lead should be moved

GYBING THE ASYMMETRIC

To gybe an asymmetric with a single sheet, come onto a run until the sail collapses in the lee of the mainsail. The sheet can then be led around the forestay, back along the other side of the boat, through the quarter block and back to the winch. But it's easier to have two sheets, and lead the lazy one around the forestay before you gybe. Let the working sheet go, and the sail will float forward and can be hauled in on the opposite gybe. If the sail is fitted with a snuffer it can be doused, and reset after the main has been gybed, the sheet has been led around the forestay and the boat has settled on the new course.

aft. You'll know the lead is good when the luff starts breaking between one-third and halfway down.

As you come further off the wind, the sheet should be eased to keep the break in the right place. Once the apparent wind comes abaft the beam, the mainsail will start to interfere with air flow to the asymmetric. Ease the tack line and the halyard to let the sail move forward away from the dirty air coming off the mainsail.

It's much easier to steer to an asymmetric than to a symmetrical kite. Come on to the wind until the luff starts to curl inwards; this means you will either have to sheet in or bear away. Take it easy, and keep course alterations gentle and unhurried. If you bear away too much, the mainsail will blanket the chute and make it collapse, and you'll need to head

Asymmetric trim tips

1 *Secret weapon: an asymmetric spinnaker can transform a slow, light-airs reach into a rip-roaring sail.*

2 *Yes, you certainly can go close to the wind with a cruising chute – as close as 40 degrees apparent – with the right sail.*

3 *These sails need to be treated with respect – they can overpower a boat if the wind gets up.*

4 *With a telescopic whisker pole, you can pole out the asymmetric's clew to run wing-and-wing.*

5 *It is more efficient to pole out the tack, as with a conventional spinnaker.*

▼ *A telescopic pole is a great help in improving downwind performance but it is best used in light airs.*

up a little, or trim the sheet, to get it working again. Experimentation is the key – take your sail out and play with it as often as possible.

Generally, when it's tacked down to the stemhead, the asymmetric will only function up to around 140 degrees from the apparent wind, which is when the main blankets it. This is why many sports boats and some cruising yachts – notably J-boats – have retractable bowsprits. They move the kite further away from the main into clear air, letting them run a few degrees further off the wind.

Instead of sailing dead downwind you will have to 'tack' downwind – sail on a broad reach up to around 140 degrees and gybe from time to time to approximate your course. The extra speed and safety – there is no chance of sailing by the lee and gybing the mainsail – should compensate for the extra distance travelled through the water.

If you want to sail at deeper angles than this, the asymmetric can be rigged with sheets and guys and its tack poled out to windward like a symmetrical spinnaker. This works reasonably well, but it's not ideal. For one thing, it's much harder to gybe than a conventional kite, as the clew needs to be freed completely and floated around the forestay to the other side of the boat. The potential for mistakes is great.

Another option is to run almost dead downwind wing and wing, with the asymmetric's clew poled out to weather. Because the asymmetric is tacked down amidships, and is as long on the foot as a symmetrical spinnaker, a normal spinnaker pole won't be long enough for this, and the best option is a telescopic pole. This rig will give much more boat-speed in light to medium airs than a poled-out genoa and is nearly as easy to set up; rig the pole with the topping lift and downhaul, run the

Sailpower

SNUFFERS

According to sailing lore, the late, great Eric Tabarly was responsible for making the spinnaker snuffer popular with cruisers. A German sailor developed the idea back in the 1960s but it wasn't until Tabarly was seen using one when he sailed his maxi yacht Pen Duick VI in the 1976 singlehanded transatlantic race that the idea caught on. Now just about every sailmaker around the globe is making them.

Snuffers have a mixed reputation. Some people swear by them, others at them. The concept is excellent – it is the execution that causes the problems. Although they all work on the same principle – an endless line runs up the sleeve, through a block at the top, and back down again – there are many variations. A poorly designed snuffer is worse than none at all, and there are a lot of bad ones around.

Many of the problems lie in the way the hoisting and return lines are routed. They tend to twist and tangle, so the snuffer gets stuck halfway and the spinnaker has to be dropped to sort out the mess. The lines need to be kept separate from the sail, ideally run in channels sewn to the inside of the sleeve. If these are made in contrasting colours, it makes twists easier to spot. If the return line is too thin it will cut into fingers when you're trying to snuff the sail in a breeze.

The sleeve itself should be made of porous open-weave cloth to cut down on friction and let trapped air out. If it's made of spinnaker nylon it tends to cling to the sail, especially when wet. It's also easy for the sleeve to twist around the spinnaker, so a quick inspection is essential to make sure that it will hoist fairly.

Big GRP 'buckets' are still found on many snuffers but these are heavy and can chafe the sailcloth, so relatively small hoop-like mouths are becoming more popular. A swivel and short pennant is connected to the spinnaker at one end and the halyard at the other to leave some clearance for the sleeve and hoop at the top of the sail. A good quality, preferably roller bearing, block for the control lines will cut down on friction. Snuffers for asymmetrical spinnakers are usually made to the length of the leech, rather than the luff, which means there is always a bit of excess cloth dangling out of the end of it. This is so the sleeve doesn't hang up on the clew ring.

Spinnaker sets with a snuffer are best accomplished the same way as with an un-snuffered sail; hoisting and dropping the snuffer with the spinnaker blanketed by the main. That way there's not so

▲ *Spinnaker snuffers can make life easier for short-handed crews.*

much chance of the sail filling with a bang with the snuffer partway up – a situation that's been responsible for many rope-burnt hands as the spinnaker forces the snuffer skywards at warp speed.

Designed and constructed properly, and used with a bit of care and attention, a snuffer can add another dimension to a sail which might otherwise spend most of its life in its bag. It's not a totally hassle-free answer, because it needs someone on the foredeck to operate the line, whereas an unsnuffered spinnaker can be set and doused without anyone having to leave the cockpit.

sheet through the pole jaws, and tie a spare sheet to the clew of the sail. Led inboard, or around the forestay this lazy sheet will help you keep some control over the sail if you have come up into the wind in a hurry. Bear in mind that telescopic poles are prone to breaking if shock loadings are put on them when they're extended, so it's best to use this rig only in light airs and flat water.

Ideally, a well set-up cruising yacht would carry both kinds of spinnaker; the symmetrical kite can't be beaten for downwind speed in light to medium airs, while the asymmetric comes into its own for power reaching. It is unreasonable to expect either sail to perform both jobs, but that's usually what happens.

10 Reefing Systems

- Slab reefing
- Single-line reefing
- Furling mainsails
- In-boom reefing

Sailpower

Slab reefing

Slab reefing is a simple and reliable system with few moving parts and therefore there is little to go wrong. Of all the mainsail reefing systems, it offers the best control over shape and trim. Because of this it remains the mainsail-shortening system of choice for most of us, and the only question is what kind of set-up to go for.

There are four common ways of setting up slab reefing.
• The clew pennants run through the boom to a winch on the mast below the gooseneck, and the tack cringle is slipped over a horn at the gooseneck.
• Clew and tack cringles are connected by a single line, which is led back to the cockpit.
• Separate clew and tack pennants are led back to the cockpit.
• The clew pennants are led back to the cockpit, while the tack cringles are hooked on to the gooseneck horn.

Three of these systems are sensible and workable in their own right. The exception is, unfortunately, the most common one; the last of those listed here. It means that someone has to go forward to do battle with unyielding folds of dacron in order to force a small cringle over an even smaller hook, then struggle back to the cockpit to winch in the clew line, all too often finding that the sail has slipped off the tack hook by the time they get there. This inevitably leads to major sense-of humour failure. So reefing usually becomes a two-person operation, with someone needed in the cockpit to harden up the halyard as soon as the sail's on the hook – all very well if there are two people on watch, but a real nuisance when short-handed.

If the whole point of leading lines aft to the cockpit is to avoid the need for anyone to go forward in the kind of conditions which necessitate taking in a reef, why do builders persist in fitting such a half-cocked set up? The simple answer is, because it's cheap. Many people have become so accustomed to this flawed system that they have developed their own techniques for coping with it, but it can be improved to a two-line system relatively inexpensively and easily.

One way is to rig a downhaul through the tack cringles. You'd need to fit a pad eye on either side of the mast, located slightly below the gooseneck fitting so when the tack is in its reefed position, the pull on it is forward and down to counteract halyard and foot tension. Tie the line to one pad eye, run it through the tack cringle and down through the other pad eye, and back to the cockpit via a block at the base of the mast. Tie the second reef line to the other pad eye and repeat the operation. If you don't want the hassle and expense of fitting extra clutches in the cockpit, you could fit a cleat on either side of the mast and make the downhauls fast to them.

You'd still need to go forward but at least you wouldn't have to hook the cringle over the reefing horn. A piece of plastic tubing over the last foot or two of the downhaul will prevent the line chafing at the cringle.

A slightly more complicated means of achieving the same end, but one that can be used to enhance general sailing performance as well, is to rig a three- or four-part tackle (handybilly) at the side of the mast.

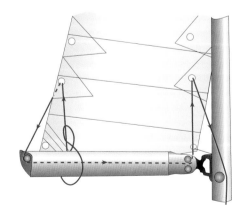

1

2

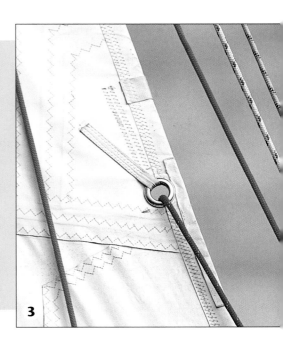

3

Reefing tips
1 *Twin hooks at the gooseneck make it easier to take in additional reefs.*
2 *A line with a stopper knot enables you to pull down a reef at the luff.*
3 *A reefing line on the leech.*

Reefing options How a single-line reef might be set up (below left); it is important that the luff be pulled down before the clew. A simple two-line system (right) might have the cunningham hook doing double duty as a tack reefing hook. This is foolproof but means working at the mast.

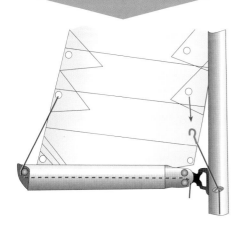

Make fast its lower block at the base of the mast and bring the tail of the tackle back to a cleat or clutch in the cockpit. Take a line from the top block through a pad eye or cheek block on the side of the mast (to ensure a good lead to the tack) and hook it to the first reef point. When it's time to reef, just haul in on the tackle as you ease the main halyard.

The disadvantages of this system are the need to go forward and relead the hook when it's time for the second reef, and the possibility of running out of purchase before the tack has been hauled down far enough – there has to be enough clearance between boom and mast base for the handybilly to pull the tack down before the two blocks run up against each other.

One advantage is that the tackle can also be used as a Cunningham to help the trim the mainsail. Another is that this tackle, and the downhaul above, can be used to winch the tack down when the boat is sailing off the wind with the mainsail drawing; a point of sail on which it is all but impossible to pull the main down by hand.

Many sparmakers offer their own variants on the two-line system. Some have the tack line running down through the hollow pin connecting gooseneck to mast, which is a neat solution.

Typically, the clew reefing pennants will be led inside the boom and, via integral jammers at the gooseneck, to a small winch on the mast beneath the gooseneck. Often, there is only room inside the boom for two reefing pennants along with the mainsail outhaul; if the mainsail has a third reef, the lines for this are often not led at all. There are two ways around this. One is to have a mainsail with two very deep reefs in it. Another is to fit external blocks for the third reef pennant, which must then be taken back to a cockpit winch and clutch.

Do you need a third reef, even if you're not going offshore? This depends on your boat. I have test-sailed many broad-sterned modern boats, designed to be sailed upright, that have been equipped with two reefs as standard, and found them annoyingly overcanvassed when trying to make to windward in winds of 25 to 30 knots, griping and breaking away when a third reef would have kept them on their feet and sailing well. Winds of this strength are far from unusual around the British Isles during the sailing season and with a well set-up boat they are no problem. With a poorly set-up reefing system they can be frightening.

Single-line reefing

Cutting the work involved in reefing down to winching in a single line is an attractive thought. Single-line reefing has become popular over the last decade and deservedly so. It means one person can take in or shake out a reef in a matter of minutes, without leaving the cockpit. Converting to this system is most easily done by buying a new boom, complete with internal blocks and pulleys. This is neat and effective, but it is not a cheap option, and may not make sense for an older boat where the shiny new boom might look incongruous.

For an older boat, it would be more cost-effective to modify the existing boom by riveting on a few judiciously placed cheek blocks on the outside of the boom. There are different ways of leading the lines, depending on the boom's design, but you will need to make sure that the tack is pulled down first. Many people have made these conversions and are happy with the result.

There are a couple of drawbacks. The most obvious is the huge amount of line that needs to be pulled through – four times the height of the reef – and ends up cluttering up the cockpit. Because the load from the clew is transferred to the tack, you will need to watch for wear in this fitting. Usually, there is only room inside the boom for two reefing lines. Then there is the inherent friction that comes from one line making so many circuitous twists and turns before it reaches the cockpit winch. This can make winching down the second reef a gruelling effort, especially with the underpowered cabintop winches usually fitted to production boats. Ball bearing blocks and sheaves go a long way towards cutting down on the hard work, but they're expensive. Fitting blocks to the clew and tack of the sail is also a good way to cut down on friction. This is increasingly being seen on bigger boats, where the loads are high, but smaller cruisers would also benefit from such attention to smooth running.

If you're prepared to spend a lot of money upgrading all the blocks, sheaves and deck organisers in the system, and don't mind being ankle-deep in line, single line reefing will be a good choice. Two-line reefing is less friction-critical but generates equal amounts of string and needs more expensive rope clutches. Your call.

> The clew reefing cringle must be pulled aft as the reef is put in, in order to act as an outhaul and flatten the sail.
>
> Whether you go with single-line or two-line reefing, friction is going to become your enemy. When it comes to hardening up the clew, you'll be fighting it every inch. It would be wise to invest in roller-bearing cheek blocks for the boom end, and also to fit one to the clew reefing cringle.

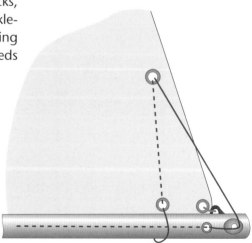

Furling mainsails

A few short years ago in-mast furling was derided by most cruising yachtsmen as fit only for pensioners and fair-weather sailors. It was unreliable and ill-performing, said its critics. Now, mainstream builders put furling mains as standard equipment on some of their boats. Large charter fleets in the Caribbean and Mediterranean scarcely have a pull-up mainsail between them. Some sparmakers reckon that 50 per cent of their output is for furling mains. What has accounted for this upsurge in popularity?

1 *The earliest furlers were just attached behind the mast, but unsupported foils tend to sag to leeward.*

2 *Many boats have been converted to in-mast furling by add-on extrusions. These work but add windage and weight.*

3 *A typical modern furling system. The spars are not noticeably bigger than conventional masts.*

Sailpower

The main reason, of course, is the indisputable simplicity and convenience of furling mainsails. Hoist it and that's that for the rest of the season. Need a reef? Ease one line, pull another. Done. None of this messing about on the coachroof pulling down the sail, flaking it properly on the boom and putting the sailcover on; with a furling main you can be off the boat and in the car (or the bar) within minutes of tying up. It all sounds very seductive, but there must be a catch...

Trim and the furling main

Furling mains are not for those who find joy in trimming, tweaking and tuning their sails and rigs. There is a price to pay for fuss-free sail handling and it is exacted in the coin of aerodynamic efficiency. The furling main's leech cannot extend beyond a straight line between clew and head, because it has no battens to support the excess cloth. Unless the leech is cut with a negative (hollow) curvature it will flutter uncontrollably. This means that compared to a battened sail of similar aspect ratio, the battenless furling main will obviously have less area – typically between 10 and 20 per cent – but its shape will punish its performance as much as the lack of area. The reason is induced drag, which results from the differential between the windward (high pressure) and leeward (low pressure) sides of the sail, especially near the top. The higher-pressure air bleeds off over the top and bottom of the sail and uses up energy which would otherwise be gainfully employed in providing lift. Sailing to windward, induced drag holds the sail back while lift drives it forward; in effect the sail is struggling with itself, and the result is increased heel and a general lack of efficiency.

Unfortunately for bermudian rigs in general and hollow-leeched mains in particular, the shape which is most susceptible to induced drag is the triangle. The elliptical trailing edge and fuller head section of a mainsail with plenty of roach is much more aerodynamically efficient, which is why you don't see many triangular wings on aircraft, or on birds. From a performance viewpoint, the more roach a sail has, the better. This concept is carried to its extreme in racing multihulls and America's Cup boats, and is only limited in cruising yachts by the need for the leech to clear the backstay when tacking.

The more the wind comes aft, the more drag works for you instead of against you and the less obvious the performance differential between the two types of mainsail, except in light airs where the extra area of a roached main is welcome.

Having started at a disadvantage by dint of its triangular shape and comparatively smaller area, the furling sail is further handicapped by the need for a flatter cut than its battened counterpart. Because the unsupported sailcloth tends to belly out – especially in the heavily loaded leech area – the sail cannot have as much camber as a battened sail, and this lack of shape limits the effects of fine-tuning.

Up to the point where the sail needs to be reefed it can be treated more or less the same as a battened sail – by adjusting the halyard tension and the kicker, the flow can be moved forward or aft, and the outhaul can be used to shape the lower part of the sail (though some furling mains we have used do not respond even to this limited tuning).

▲ *Without battens, an in-mast furling mainsail cannot support any roach and thus has less area than an equivalent battened sail.*

One of the benefits of furling mains is the way they allow you to reef in small increments to balance the boat.

The lack of roach makes it hard to get any twist into the sail, so its upper parts stall more easily; this can lead to lee helm going upwind in light conditions. It is not uncommon for boats that have been converted to inmast furling to need their headsail cut down in size in order to eliminate the lee helm.

Once even one or two rolls have been taken in the sail, tensioning the halyard has no effect (except to strain the head ring, sheave and top swivel) because the sailcloth will be binding against the foil. As with a genoa, technique is a key factor in determining how good the set of a reefed sail will be. The instinctive tendency is to keep some tension on the outhaul line to stop the sail from flogging as it is rolled away. This puts the leech and foot under more tension than the middle of the sail, which will roll away more loosely than the ends, and as the sail passes through the slot in the mast it tends to crease and bunch up. This results in a bulkier roll on the foil, which makes the furler difficult to operate, and it is not unusual for it to jam the sail against the sides of the mast extrusion so that it won't budge at all.

Insufficient luff tension also makes for too much camber in the sail. As the wind gets up, the draft moves further aft, causing drag, and the boat gets slow and cranky.

For an efficient furl the leech needs to be completely unloaded. This is best achieved by topping the boom up a little above horizontal, easing the mainsheet and freeing off the outhaul to let the sail feather while you put in the desired number of rolls. With no load on the sail it'll be much quicker and easier to operate the furling gear, and topping up the boom ensures that the thick seams at the foot roll up helicoil fashion – if they overlay one another they may well jam up the sail before it's all rolled away.

Using this technique it's possible to get the reefed sail setting nearly as flat as a battened main, and in heavier going where the main needs to be eased down the traveller to balance out weather helm and it's not possible to point high anyway, a well-reefed furling main can perform well. While a slab reefing main might find itself in a situation where one reef is not enough and two is too many, the furler's ability to reef in tiny increments makes it easier to match sail area to wind and sea conditions.

Something else to bear in mind is that where it is often possible to reef conventional sails on a reach or a run (as long as they have low-friction luff fittings), the wind pressure pushing the furling sail against the lip of the mast slot creates so much friction that you need to come well up into the wind to feather the sail before you can start rolling it away.

Adding battens

Many fine minds have busied themselves trying to marry the convenience and neatness of the in-mast furling concept to the power and efficiency of a well-shaped mainsail. All have concluded that roach – which means battens – is what's needed to woo performance-minded yachtsmen over to the furling concept, so plenty of variations on this theme have been tried over the years. A Swedish inventor thought pneumatic battens were the way to go and demonstrated the concept at an Earls Court show. Enthusiasm for the idea quickly waned on sight of the foot pump which had to be placed in the cockpit to inflate the battens as they appeared from the mast, and the expense and complexity of fitting the air lines to the batten ends applied the coup de grace to that scheme.

Short vertical battens going partway down the sail can be seen on some bigger boats, where the weight penalty is not so noticeable, but they have not come into widespread use on smaller yachts because they are not able to support any roach. At best they allow the leech to be cut in a straight line. Yet another system has battens consisting of pairs of opposing concave strips like tape measure sections, which flatten against each other as the sail is rolled away. It is not unheard of for these sections to spring open inside the mast and jam the sail in place.

MAKING LIFE EASIER

Lazyjacks
In the context of improving a reefing set-up, lazyjacks are a good way of avoiding the need to tie in reef points to keep the bunt of the sail from flapping about, restricting your field of view and generally being a nuisance. They are a boon for shorthanded crews or solo sailors. Well set-up lazyjacks should have a minimum of three 'legs' per side, otherwise the sail won't be contained properly. They can chafe the stitching on the sail too, so it's a good idea to set them up so they can be taken to the mast and hooked out of the way while you're hoisting the sail. If you do that, you'll also avoid the annoying tendency of your full-length battens to catch in the lazyjacks. It can take a lot of trial and error to come up with a lazyjack system that works the way it should.

The Dutchman system
This is popular in the USA and is also available in the UK. A second topping lift is fitted, and from it a number of long, thin lines are threaded through grommets in the sail and fastened at the boom. When the sail is dropped or reefed the lines hold it in place so it doesn't sag off the boom. Critics of the system point out the potential for chafe, but its advocates say that this is not a big problem. Fitting the sail cover around all the lines is more of a nuisance. The Dutchman system works best with softer, short-battened sails.

Sail bags

The Doyle Stack-Pack was the forerunner of these increasingly common systems, all variations on the same theme: a permanent sail cover is fitted to the boom, the sail drops into it, and it is zipped up. It's a neat and simple way of putting the sail to bed. Problems? Keeping zippers working when they get gummed up with salt, and increased windage. Chafe could also be a factor, and sailmakers aren't keen on them – 'you don't really want a bag flapping around rubbing on your sail,' said one. They aren't suitable for boats over 40ft or so, where the booms are so high that it's difficult to zip up the cover.

▶ *When furling the sail it is best to let it feather. This mainsail has vertical battens.*

In the mid-1990s Swedish sailmaker Peter Lundh came up with the Vertech system. Its closely spaced vertical battens are made of 10mm thick interconnecting hollow rods, GRP in the lower sections and carbon fibre at the top where extra stiffness is needed to support the highly loaded leech.

Vertech allows the sail to carry as much roach as a conventional horizontally-battened main, and potentially more than that, though Lundh is still developing the system and is careful not to make exaggerated claims. It is expensive, in part because of the construction and also because it demands a high quality sailcloth with plenty of bias stability (most polyester weaves are strong in the warp and fill directions, but prone to stretch when loads are applied on the bias – at an angle to the thread directions). If the wrong cloth is used, a vertically battened sail will stretch between the batten tops.

Having tried both Vertech and Maxi-Roach mainsails, I can vouch for the fact that the sail shape was a definite improvement over an unbattened mainsail. The sails are almost identical in area to a conventional fully-battened main, and performed well to windward. The cut still needs to be flatter than you might like to see in light airs, but it will hold its shape much better as the wind increases.

The makers claim that the battens make reefing more efficient because they act as reef points and eliminate any tendency for the sail to crease along the luff as it is being rolled away. The support along the leech also dampens the flogging when the outhaul is eased to reef the sail.

The technology is beginning to be more widely adopted by other lofts in Europe and seems certain to become commonplace. It is the best solution so far to the question of getting decent performance out of a furling main.

The way ahead?

Considering the universal enthusiasm with which the cruising community has embraced roller furling headsails, and mankind's natural desire for an easier life, perhaps the only surprise is that it has taken so long for in-mast furling to reach its present level of acceptance. It has made it possible for small crews to handle big boats safely, and kept many people sailing who physically would no longer be able to handle conventional mainsails.

Not that the picture is entirely rosy. Although the furling systems are much more reliable than they used to be, sail jams can occur, and few people would feel happy going blue-water cruising with in-mast furling unless a track to carry a trysail was added to the mast. It would also be wise to look closely into the boat's stability characteristics before opting for in-mast furling, especially if there are plans to go offshore. The extra weight aloft of the foil and reefed sail raises the boat's centre of gravity and, especially when combined with one or more furling headsails – plus radomes and radar reflectors – will affect its righting moment. The significance of this varies according to the design parameters of the boat.

Those who are thinking of retrofitting in-mast furling might also consider that the reduction in mainsail area can unbalance the sailplan and cause lee helm, so that the genoa may need to be cut down in size, with a consequence loss of light-airs performance.

In-boom reefing

In-boom reefing is nothing more than a refinement of the good old-fashioned boom roller reefing method that was common until relatively recently. In most of these systems a geared mechanism worked through the mast via a universal joint to the gooseneck to rotate the boom. As the sail was rolled away, someone in the cockpit usually had to pull on the leech to keep the sail from bunching up at the luff.

It had its good points, in that the load on the sail was distributed along the length of the reef and therefore kinder than slab reefing to cotton sails, and the sail area could be reduced or increased in increments, thus making it easier to balance the boat. On the downside, halyard tension had to be carefully controlled, and the kicking strap and mainsheet tackles had to be mounted on 'claws' that let the boom and sail rotate within their grasp. The end of the boom always drooped when reefed unless the boom was wider aft than at the front. Nor was it possible to use an outhaul, so the reefed sail usually was too full.

Modern boom reefing involves a rotating spar inside the boom around which the sail is rolled. Around ten years ago there was a minor boom (sorry) in these systems; Danish company Sailtainer and Hood with its Stoboom made a valiant effort to re-establish in-boom reefing but ran into the same problems which have plagued other manufacturers – the difficulty of keeping the boom at a constant angle in a seaway. Unless it was held at an exact angle, the sail's boltrope wouldn't roll up properly, leading to foul-ups inside the boom. The problem was exacerbated by the compression loads from fully-battened sails, which made the sails difficult to hoist. Accelerated wear on the boltrope and luff tape was also a major problem.

There are now a number of in-boom systems which allow the use of full-length battens and sails with a normal amount of roach, which makes for a much better shape. Most have articulated sail tracks which permit the reefing system to be operated without the need to come head-to-wind, which is a big bonus on a cruising boat. The pivoting tracks also cut down on luff tape wear, which was a curse that affected earlier attempts at this technology. Still, it is critical to keep the boom at

▲ *An early Profurl in-boom system, showing how the sail can have a normal amount of roach.*

REEFING PROTOCOL

Let me start by saying that you should not need to come head-to-wind in order to reef. If your mainsail can only be coaxed down when the wind's on the nose then you need to pay some attention to the luff slides or batten cars.

• If you want to keep the boat moving when reefing, come off the wind onto a reach and trim the headsail to suit. The autopilot will steer the boat better and the motion won't be so pronounced.

• Harden up on the topping lift – this will stop the boom from dropping when the halyard is released.

• Ease off the kicking strap to take the pressure off the mainsail leech. If you have a solid kicker, you needn't worry about taking up on the topping lift.

• Dump the mainsheet to depower the sail.

• Free the halyard and pull down the luff of the sail until the tack ring can be placed over the reefing horn on the boom.

• Harden up on the halyard.

• Winch in the clew pennant until the clew fitting is just clear of the boom.

• Ease the topping lift, trim the mainsheet and harden up on the kicker.

If you're sailing shorthanded, it can be a good idea to heave-to in order to reef. This is a great way to take the sting out of a big wind and sea, and will give you plenty of time to do the work before gybing around to resume your course. Another good thing to do is to fit a piece of webbing with a ring at either end to the tack fitting. The rings will be easier to fit over the reefing horn.

If you have lazyjacks, you probably won't need to think about tying in the reef points. I've seldom bothered with this unless there has been some shock cord on board; I have twice seen a mainsail badly ripped, once because someone forgot the reef points were in when they tried to shake out a reef, the second time when a clew pennant parted; the main would have been unharmed had the reef points not been tied. Since then I've always looped a sail tie around the boom and through the clew a couple of times, just for peace of mind. If you must tie the reef points, use shock cord.

The crew of this boat has decided to heave-to in order to take in a reef.

a precise angle to the sail track in order to get the sail to roll up properly, so a rigid kicker pre-set to the right height is essential. There is a lot of friction in these systems, and in boats over 40 feet, powered winches are often fitted to assist in setting the sail. There is also a weight penalty of up to 40 per cent over a standard boom, but at least the weight and that of the furled sail is kept low, unlike an in-mast system.

Retro-fitting a furling boom to a boat is not a cheap operation, although it may be possible to adapt the existing mainsail, and is best left to a professional. The cost is not cheap and there are still question marks about their long-term reliability and suitability for ocean voyaging, although the fact that they can be lowered even if the furling mechanism failed is a strong point in their favour. Having the sailmaker add reef points to a furling sail as a failsafe would be a good idea for those venturing offshore with a furling boom.

99

11 Strong Wind Sailing

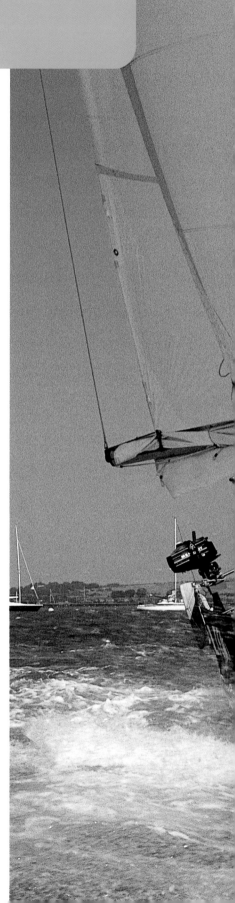

Trim first – then reef

Storm sails

The trysail

Sailing in a good blow can be either exhilarating or frightening; knowing how your boat responds to sail trim and reefing, and when to think about storm canvas, can make all the difference. As much as the wind strength, sea conditions will dictate sail trim and reefing. In flat water, you could sail all day under full sail with the toerail skimming the water and have a whale of a time. It's a different story when you're beating into a nasty chop inshore or bigger seas offshore.

As the wind builds, the object is to keep the boat well balanced, ie sailing at maximum efficiency to windward with as little weather helm as possible. The typical 1980s/90s cruiser has an asymmetrical, unbalanced waterplane, with a lot of beam aft in order to fit in the requisite aft cabin and large cockpit. This hull shape is fast and fun to sail in light to medium airs, but when it comes on to blow it suffers by comparison with more traditional hull forms. It likes to be sailed fairly upright. The more it heels, the more unbalanced the underwater shape becomes, and the more weight there'll be on the helm.

Trim first – then reef

I will start by saying that it is much better to reef early than reef late, but it is fun – and also important – to find out exactly how far your boat can be pressed before she starts to misbehave. A good strong wind and flat water are ideal for experimentation. Your goal is to minimise the heeling while retaining as much drive as possible. You will need to flatten both sails as much as possible and get the draft well forward in them. On a masthead rig, crank on plenty of backstay tension if possible in order to tighten the forestay and prevent the genoa luff from sagging, which will make the sail fuller – the last thing you want in a stiff breeze. Hardening up on the backstay should also have the effect of tensioning the halyard,

Sailing to weather under reefed headsail in a blow. In conditions like these, it pays to keep the main as flat as possible.

Sailpower

moving the draft forward in the headsail. The sheet should be just cracked, until the leech is six inches or so clear of the shrouds. The sheet lead can be moved aft a stop or two to let the top of the sail twist off and open up the leech, which will help keep the boat on its feet.

The tight backstay should help to flatten the upper part of the mainsail – this effect will be much more pronounced on a fractional rig. The main halyard should also be tensioned until the draft is about 45 per cent back from the luff, and the outhaul needs to be tightened so the bottom of the sail is flat. To get rid of the weather helm, gradually ease the traveller down the track to leeward. The main will soon start to backwind, but don't worry; this will reduce weather helm and since the genoa is the driving sail to windward, it won't affect speed. The main should backwind evenly; if the top goes first, there is too much twist in the sail, so it needs to be sheeted in a bit; if the bottom luffs first, ease the sheet to put some twist in. If there is too much backwinding, the slot between jib and mainsail may be too tight, so ease the jibsheet a little or trim the main.

Eventually, the boat will heel to a point where it will become seriously unbalanced unless you shorten sail. On a typical modern cruiser, with its fine bows and generous beam carried all the way aft to a broad stern, this point can arrive at around 15 and often by 20 degrees of heel. If it heels much more, the rudder may be lifted far enough out of the water to lose its grip and the boat will round up uncontrollably into the wind. A more old-fashioned hull form, with narrower beam and longer overhangs, may be able to cope with heel angles of 35 degrees or more without misbehaving. Even so, it will be a lot more comfortable under shortened sail; it is time to reef.

So, which sail should be reefed first? All boats are different and you'll have to experiment to find out which sail combinations best suit your boat. As a rule of thumb, the sail closest to the wind should be reduced first. If you are going to windward and the mainsail is reefed first, the centre of effort will move forward and the boat may develop lee helm while still feeling overpressed; then you will have to reef the headsail to balance the helm, which may leave you undercanvassed.

On boats with big (140-150 per cent) overlapping genoas, rolling away enough to leave the clew level with the shrouds should balance the boat very nicely. If the main is flattened as much as possible, with plenty of luff and outhaul tension (and plenty of backstay tension if it is a fractional rig), you should be able to carry a full main into quite a high wind speed.

Off the wind, reefing the mainsail first will offset the boat's desire to luff up and let you steer a straighter course without fighting the helm.

It is not an uncommon practice to drop one sail or another when the wind gets up quickly. Which one should you leave up? It is always easy to roll the headsail away and pound along under mainsail only. As long as you don't expect to point higher than a close reach, this is fine. If you do decide to jog along under headsail alone, bear in mind that in strong winds and lumpy seas there will be a large compression load on the masthead and consequently a lot of stress on the mast. With no mainsail to counteract the pressure, there is a possibility that the mast could invert – bend aft and collapse. This is much less likely to happen if there is some prebend in the mast, as in a fractional rig, or, in the case

TACTICAL BEATING

In a fair and just world you'd be taking the seas at a 45 degree angle on each tack but it never seems to work out that way. On one tack you'll be driving almost head-on into the seas, on the other taking them more on the beam. On the nasty tack the boat labours through the seas, slamming and pitching. On the other she'll feel livelier and more responsive, making better ground to windward. Yet the sail trim is the same on both tacks. What is going wrong?

You're having trouble because the wave train seldom follows the wind direction exactly. It is not unusual to have the wind blowing 20 or 30 degrees across the direction of the seas, especially as a low-pressure system passes overhead. You just have to live with it. On the awkward tack, you will make better progress by sailing five or ten degrees lower, giving up some VMG in favour of higher boatspeed and a more comfortable ride.

of a masthead rig, the spar is fitted with forward lowers or a babystay. The strength of the spar is also a factor.

Unless the boat is leaping off the waves and landing with a jarring crash, it should be safe to sail under headsail alone, but most riggers would counsel against it. Sailing under a double-reefed mainsail is probably a more sensible option.

Storm sails

▲ Storm jibs generally suffer from under-employment. On this one the hanks have seized up.

What's orange, never comes out of its bag and lives right at the bottom of the cockpit locker? Right, the storm jib. Most yachts have one, but few have ever been used in anger. When we're caught out in a blow, the usual procedure is to roll the headsail up to hanky size and make for port. This usually works out pretty well, until the wind gets above force 8. Roller headsails weren't designed to work in 45-50 knots of wind and those conditions will soon winkle out any weaknesses in your furling gear too. I've seen a genoa unfurl itself in 40 knots when a furling line broke and it nearly shook the mast out of the boat.

Having decided that it's a good idea to have a storm jib, the question remains of how to get it up there when you need it, short of dropping the genoa and hoisting it on the forestay – and doing that in 40 knots of wind is hardly practical, let alone safe. If the genoa has to stay in place, what's the best way of setting the storm jib, bearing in mind that the job should be able to be done by one person in the minimum of time, and that the storm jib should set well enough to let you make ground to weather?

Some years ago I was involved in a *Yachting Monthly* practical exercise in which we tried out a handful of different approaches to this problem. The exercise took place in fairly flat water, in 35-40 knots of wind; not quite the conditions in which you'd usually contemplate setting up the storm jib, but close enough.

One of these bright ideas involved wrapping a two-ply jib around the rolled-up genoa and tying the clews together – it took two people on the foredeck to rig the flapping beast, and although it set well on the wind, downwind the two plies wanted to separate and go wing-and-wing. It was one of those ideas that looked good on paper.

Another had a sleeve stitched to the jib which was passed around the forestay and clipped back on itself – it took ages, but again set very well once it was up. A third was laced to the forestay, and had a good shape once it was up, but again involved a time-consuming chore pitching up and down while clinging to the forestay. All of these operations would have been most unpleasant, and not a little risky, in a rough seaway.

At any rate, the forestay is often not the best place for a storm jib, especially set over a rolled-up sail. The windage forward will blow the bows off and seriously impair windward progress. The storm sail ideally should be closer to the mast, where it will balance the boat better in tandem with triple-reefed main or trysail. Many offshore cruising boats have a demountable wire stay fitted to the mast, running to a strong point on the foredeck and tensioned by a wheeled adjuster – it's hard to get enough tension with a Highfield lever. There must some way of securing the stay tightly against the shrouds or mast when it's not in use or it'll bang around in the rigging and generally be a nuisance. The deck eye must be securely fixed to a structural bulkhead, or supported by a tensioner connected to the hull.

If the stay is fixed too low on the mast, so it's not supported by the backstay, it could cause the mast to start pumping. Setting up and tensioning the wire stay can be a long and awkward process, and the mast fitting needs to be strong. Against that, being able to hank on a jib from a wider, safer part of the foredeck, and in the process bringing the sail's centre of effort closer to the mast, is no bad thing.

Another method that works well is to take the spinnaker halyard down to the foredeck eye and hank the storm jib to it. Luff tension is provided by the storm jib's wire luff, and the halyard is just used as a guide to stop the sail from blowing downwind as you're setting it. You'll need a second spinnaker or spare genoa halyard to hoist the jib with, but having a spare halyard fitted is a good idea for all sorts of reasons. It's also a good idea to leave a set of sheets permanently attached to the storm jib, and get a clear idea of where its leads will be.

There's no easy answer to the storm jib conumdrum; you can either go for a convenient solution which means spending the minimum of time on the foredeck, or a more elaborate operation which will give you better performance to windward. The best compromise is the cutter rig, which lets you set storm sails on the permanently rigged inner forestay.

▲ *A spinnaker halyard can be used as a forestay for the storm jib.*

The trysail

The number of yachtsmen who have used a storm jib is legion compared to those who have had to use a trysail in anger. You could sail for a lifetime without running into conditions that are too much for a triple-reefed mainsail. There is little point in the average coastal cruiser carrying a trysail, but most ocean cruisers wouldn't leave port without one – 'just in case'. Better to blow out a relatively cheap trysail than an expensive main; it's also nice to have a backup in case the mainsail and/or boom is damaged.

◀ *It's easier to hoist a trysail if you have a separate luff track.*

At around 33 per cent of the mainsail's area, about the same size as the third reef, the trysail is usually made of a slightly heavier cloth than the mainsail. It is cut flat, with a hollow leech to minimise flogging. Its tack will be cut high to enable it to fit over a flaked mainsail. Its head should be hoisted to the first spreader, or where its pull can be counteracted by the forward lowers or babystay. Like any other sail, it needs to be easy to set up; if it's not, it won't get used, or someone could get hurt in the attempt. It needs its own dedicated track. I've seen some that are supposed to feed into the mainsail's luff groove and this is a really unsatisfactory setup; you'd need to take some of the mainsail slides out, and then try to feed the trysail into the mainsail's luff groove while standing at the mast. Anybody who recommends that can't have tried it bouncing around in 40 knots of wind.

The track should extend past the boom to within two feet of the deck, so the whole operation can be done from a seated position. Some trysails have a wire tack pennant, which will chafe the daylights out of your mainsail, and this should be replaced with a rope strop, maybe of one of the ultra-tough high-tech lines

REEFING THE HEADSAIL

Getting a roller furling headsail to 'reef' properly is a perennial headache. As it's rolled up, the part of the sail that contains the most material – the middle – gets progressively fuller so that the sail ends up with a sizeable 'belly' in it, just when you want it to be as flat as possible. This is aggravated if the sail is rolled up with tension on the leech and foot because the wind pushes on the middle of the sail. If you just ease the sheet to let the sail feather while quickly rolling away a few turns, you'll end up with a flatter sail.

If you need a winch to roll away the headsail, then something is wrong with either the furling gear or the lead of the furling line. Most production boats leave the factory with the cheapest possible deck gear on them and a big improvement can be achieved by upgrading to low-friction blocks and paying some attention to the furling line leads.

Don't forget that the sheet leads will need to be moved forward as the sail is progressively reefed. It's a good idea to mark the reef points on the sail, then work out the best position for the sheet leads for each 'reef' and mark them next to the sheet track, either with indelible marker or dabs of paint.

No matter how well a heavily reefed headsail sets – nowhere near as well as a no. 4 jib, that's for sure – there'll come a time when there is just too much wind to carry it. The windage of the rolled-up sail will blow the bows off. This is the time to think about storm sails.

▲ *Roller-reefing a genoa is marginally less efficient than changing to a smaller headsail, but for cruising skippers that's a small price to pay.*

Sailpower

like Spectra. The slides too should be lashed loosely to the sail or they'll bind on the way up the track. The track must have a stop at the top to prevent the sail from disappearing into thin air if the tack strop breaks or comes adrift.

The trysail can be sheeted to the end of the boom, in which case you'll need to use the outhaul line or one of the mainsail's leech reefing pennants as the clew outhaul on the trysail; the mainsheet is then used to control the trysail. Another way is to sheet the sail to the quarters, taking the sheets to the primary winches via a pair of snatchblocks. Some people recommend that the boom be lowered and lashed out of the way, but to do that you may have to take some of the lower mainsail slides out of the luff groove or at least free the outhaul.

The decision of whether to sheet to the boom end or the quarters may be decided by something as trivial as the kicker – if you have a rod or gas vang fitted you'd have to disconnect it to drop the boom – or boom height; on many smaller centre cockpit yachts, the boom is carried so high that it wouldn't be possible to sheet the trysail to the quarters.

▲ If you're prepared for it and know how to handle your boat, sailing in a strong breeze is exhilarating.

Either way, lazyjacks will need to be taken forward to the mast, and there is the question of what to do with the topping lift if the boom is lowered to the deck. It's worth experimenting with both methods to see which works on your boat. One important point that could tip the scales in favour of a boom-end setup is that a trysail can flog violently and the flailing sheets could be a danger to the crew.

As part of the spring work-up, or when introducing new crew to the boat, you would do well to take the opportunity to run the storm jib up (ten to one the hanks will have seized up) and, if you have one, the trysail too. Make sure you know how the sheet leads are set up, how high to hoist the sail, and mark the tack pennants to suit. Practice lashing the boom to the deck, and work out what will get in the way. It'll be an edifying exercise. If nothing else, the operation will convince you of the wisdom of reeving the leech pennant for the third reef, and strengthen your resolve never to miss another early-morning shipping forecast.

12 Cutters, Ketches and Yawls

The cutter

Ketches and yawls

The cutter

Of the assorted ways of dividing a boat's sailplan into smaller, more easily handled chunks, the cutter is much the simplest. There is only one mast to think about but three sails to play with. Pedantically speaking, a true cutter will have its mast stepped nearly amidships, or at least 40 per cent of waterline length abaft the bows, with a consequently smaller mainsail and larger foretriangle than a sloop, and will have two or even three headsails, the foremost of which is stayed to a bowsprit. The mast would be shorter than a sloop's of the same size. In reality, the only defining criteria these days are the multiple headsails. More often than not, the cutter rig is offered as an option on a boat that is designed to carry a single overlapping headsail and so has a mast located further forward than that of a 'true' cutter. Sometimes a short bowsprit is added to extend the foretriangle to 'classic' cutter proportions, and to allow a bigger staysail to be carried than would be the case.

Configuration

As a rule of thumb, the inner forestay is fixed to the deck about a quarter of the way back from the forestay, and secured a similar distance down from the masthead, usually at the top spreaders. It needs to be supported by running backstays which are led to a point abaft the aft lower shrouds.

Sailpower

◄ *The cutter makes a popular cruising boat because the sail area is divided into smaller, more easily-managed chunks; several sizes of headsail can be set and are relatively easy to change, depending on the weather. Here the combination of reefed mainsail, jib and staysail concentrate the sail amidships, putting less stress on the rig.*

The cutter traditionally carries a yankee jib with minimal overlap, while a non-overlapping staysail is set on the inner stay. The classic yankee is cut with a very high clew to minimise twist, so that there is no need to move the sheet leads forward when the sheet is eased for off-wind sailing. The modern double-headsail sloop tends to have a jib with a high-cut clew and a certain amount of overlap. These make much better roller-furling headsails than do low-cut genoas; the angle between the sheet and the middle of the forestay hardly changes as the sail is rolled, obviating the need to adjust the leads. Another point in favour of the yankee derivative as a cruising sail is that it's easy to see under the high clew. A sail similar in cut to the yankee is used by offshore racing crews, who call it a jib top or a reacher and set it when close-reaching because it sheets more effectively and doesn't scoop up water like a deck-sweeping genoa.

The staysail sheet leads will be further inboard than the yankee's, which, at least on older designs, will be either on the toerail or close to it. Staysails are typically cut fairly flat for good windward performance, and built of a heavier cloth and with a fairly high clew so they can be carried into quite strong winds; many cutter owners have never had to set a storm jib.

Windward sailing

Aerodynamically, the cutter sailplan is not so efficient to windward as a single headsail. It can be difficult to trim the double headsails to make them work together; if the yankee is sheeted in too hard it will choke the staysail. All things being equal, a sloop should outsail a cutter to windward in light to moderate airs. There is more to sailing than the ability to point high though, and the cutter really starts to shine when the sea and wind start to build. Where a sloop rig has one slot between headsail and main for the wind to accelerate through, the cutter has two, and they generate a lot of drive, which is just what you want for beating into a rough sea. Eased off to a reach, the cutter rig generates huge amounts of power. When the wind falls light, though, it is good to have a big gennaker or MPS on standby.

Crew-kindly

The flexibility of the cutter can only really be appreciated when you've sailed one. The split foretriangle is kind to the crew. I remember without fondness the drudgery of headsail changes on big sloops in pre-roller furling days; two or three crew wrestling the genoa into submission, unhanking, bagging and dragging the big sail back to the cockpit, then going through the process in reverse to get the number two or three up.

In contrast, on the cutter I owned, 90 per cent of foredeck work involved merely hauling down either the yankee or the staysail but leaving them hanked on, lashing the former to the guardrails or stuffing the latter in its bag, and scurrying thankfully back to the cockpit. One person could do it

▼ *The versatile cutter sailing under staysail and main, it is well balanced and a pleasure to handle.*

and she was not a small boat. Only rarely did we have to change a sail and that was usually in light winds. With one or both sails set on furling gears, the workload would be minimal, ideal for a cruising couple.

By switching between the two headsails and reefing the main, a cutter can be balanced very well to cope with changing wind and sea conditions. When it really comes on to blow, the combination of staysail and reefed main concentrates sail around the middle of the boat, which puts a lot less stress on the rig and lets you make ground to windward much better than the sloop combination of reefed main and partly-rolled genoa. Localising the sailplan's centre of effort close to amidships also reduces pitching in big seas. Because a true cutter's mast is located closer to amidships, the shroud base can be wider, so the mast section and standing rigging can be made a little lighter, which means less weight aloft.

A staysail can be carried into the sort of wind that would call for a storm jib on a sloop with a roller furling headsail, and when things get really bad you can hand the mainsail and sail under staysail alone; it will not put the same compression loads on the mast as a jib set on the outer forestay.

▼ *A big cruising ketch waits for the wind; this rig has fallen out of favour although it has much going for it.*

Most cutters heave-to beautifully under reefed main and staysail, where a partly rolled genoa tends to pull the bows too far off the wind. If a storm jib needs to be substituted for the staysail, then this job can be carried out more safely in the middle of the deck than in the bows.

The fact that cutters are usually equipped with running backstays is often considered a mark against them, but to be honest it is not a big deal. There is seldom a need to use the runners except to counteract the pull of the staysail and stop the mast from pumping when beating into a rough sea. Most of the time – all of the time if the boat is being sailed as a sloop – they can be left clipped to deck eyes by the shrouds where they won't interfere with the mainsail.

And the disadvantages?

So, if the cutter is such a marvellous rig, why is it not more common? Probably because it's unwieldy in the sort of conditions and locations in which most of us sail. Coaxing the headsail between the stays while tacking is a pain, especially if the stay-sail is hanked on. Sailcloth and sheets get caught on the hanks and chafe can be a problem (a good trick is to

Cutters, Ketches and Yawls

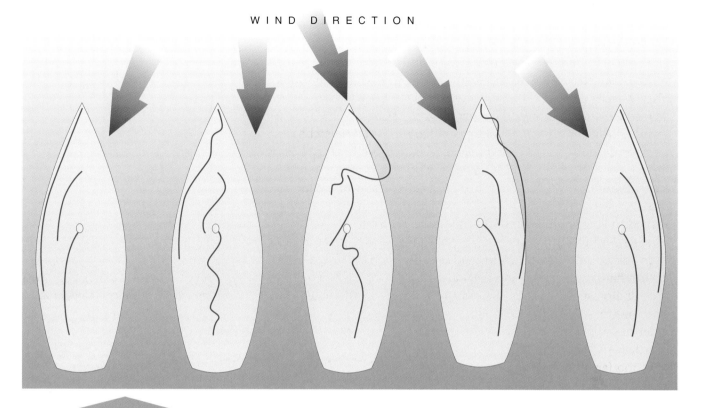

Tacking a double-headsail rig. It is often better to leave the staysail aback; as well as helping to push the bow through the wind, it will be much easier for the headsail to slide across it.

leave the staysail aback to help the headsail slide across it, then tack it once the headsail has been trimmed). There are two sets of sheets and winches to deal with (although because the sails are smaller than a single overlapping headsail, the loadings are lighter). For coastal and inshore sailing, where manoeuvrability is important, the sloop is easier to handle, and its overlapping genoa is easier to trim and will provide better drive in most conditions. The cutter's twin headsails are also at a disadvantage sailing off the wind in light airs, when the staysail contributes virtually nothing and the yankee's lack of area becomes a handicap.

For these reasons, a typical modern cutter might have a furling genoa and an overlap of 120 degrees or so, and a detachable inner forestay, so that she can be sailed as a sloop for day-to-day pottering. Many staysails are made self-tacking, often set on a boom. While there is little reason to not have the yankee set on a furling gear, there is a good argument for having the staysail hanked on as a safety measure, simply because of its importance as a heavy weather sail. Furling gears are pretty reliable but they can go wrong, and in truth, working well back from the bows in comparative safety, it is no hardship to drop or set a hanked staysail.

Ketches and yawls

Twenty or thirty years ago most boatbuilders offered ketch rigs as options on some of their boats, even quite small ones; witness the Laurent Giles-designed 31ft Westerlys. The popular 30ft Nantucket Clipper, designed by Alan Buchanan, had a yawl rig and sold by the score. Now it is rare to see production builders offer ketches at all, and of those available very few are smaller than 50ft long, while the yawl has virtually disappeared.

Sailpower

Where have all the ketches and yawls gone?

The main reasons for their decline are changes in yacht design and the improvement in sail handling technology. With roller-furling headsails, in-mast or in-boom furling mainsails, more efficient self-tailing or powered winches and low-friction blocks, even quite big sloops are now easy for a couple to work, so there is not the incentive to split up the sailplan and make the sails smaller and easier to handle. It is also cheaper to build a boat with one mast than two.

Changes in racing rules, which have always influenced cruising yacht design, also played a part in the gradual decline of the two-masted cruising boat. For many years the RORC and Cruising Club of America

The 1960s Cowes classic yawl Kataree *making the most of her sail area in light airs. The small mizzen makes a good site for the radome.*

(CCA) rules favoured two masts by rating the mizzen sail area lightly and considering the mizzen staysail to be unrated sail area. Thus yawls especially proliferated in the 1950s and '60s. This happy state of affairs came to an abrupt end with the introduction of the International Offshore Rule (IOR) in the 1970s. Along with leading hull design down a few blind alleys, the IOR effectively killed off the development of two-masted rigs for many years.

It's all about the mizzen

The traditional difference between a ketch and a yawl is that a yawl's mizzen is stepped abaft the rudderpost, so putting it further away from the mainsail, but the relative sizes of their mizzens is a more obvious distinction. A yawl is basically a sloop or cutter with a miniscule mizzen, usually 10 to 15 per cent of total sail area, while a ketch usually has its mainmast stepped a little further forward with a smaller foretriangle to compensate for the extra sail area – as much as 50 per cent of main/foretriangle area – added by its large mizzen.

Modern yacht design has also played a part in the extinction of the yawl. Overhangs have become progressively shorter and on most modern boats, the rudder is located directly under the transom, leaving nowhere to put a mizzen. Split rigs also work better with longish keels, where the ability to juggle sail area at both ends of the boat is useful to balance the helm, while the typical 1990s cruiser or cruiser-racer has a high-aspect fin.

Another reason for the fall from grace of the small ketch is that all too often the mizzen was put slap bang in the middle of the cockpit, where it got in everyone's way and the downdraught from the sail went straight down the helmsman's collar. On some ketches it's not possible to use self-steering gear because of interference from the mizzen boom, which is a nuisance if you're planning ocean voyaging.

Because luff length is important in windward performance, ketches and yawls, with their low-aspect ratio sailplans, are generally not as efficient upwind as taller, single-masted rigs. For a mizzen to provide extra lift and useful windward performance, it must be stepped sufficiently clear of the mainsail. The relationship between mizzen and main is critical and can lead to plenty of trimming headaches; if the two are set too close together, the wind accelerates along the lee side of the mainsail and backwinds the mizzen. This annoys you to the extent that you tend to oversheet the mizzen, which leads to weather helm. To get rid of the weather helm, you drop the mizzen, and then the extra mast and rigging provide nothing but dead weight and drag.

Windward ability is only a small part of the picture, though. Two-masted rigs are powerful and easy to handle when sheets are eased, and this is why they will always be popular with the blue-water fraternity where those last few degrees of closewindedness are seldom relevant. With three or four sails up on a reach, the slot effect really comes into its own and the mizzen becomes part of the overall sailplan instead of an individual mast. With a mizzen staysail backing up a cruising chute, a ketch can leave a single-master trailing in its wake. The mizzen staysail is a terrific sail, effective with the wind just forward of

Sailpower

the beam to a broad reach. It's easy to set and douse because you don't need to leave the cockpit (it's even easier if fitted with a furler), and when combined with the smaller spinnaker of a ketch it makes for an easily controlled downwind powerhouse. From a very broad reach to run it is best to drop the mizzen, as it'll be blanketing the mainsail. In a blow, you can drop the mainsail and jolly along or heave-to under staysail and mizzen – 'jib and jigger' – and a suitably reefed mizzen can be used as a riding sail at anchor.

SCHOONERS

There are few logical reasons to own a schooner. They go like the clappers on a reach if you fill the big gap between those masts with things like fishermen, gollywobblers and staysails. The huge mainsail is hard to handle and you wouldn't want to crash-gybe it. Schooners are inefficient to windward. On the other hand, they look lovely, and if all your sailing is going to be in trade wind conditions, why not? Otherwise, leave them to the traditionalists.

Plus points

Ketches and yawls have other, less obvious attributes. A divided sailplan distributes rig stresses more evenly along the hull. The mizzen makes an ideal place to hang wind generators, radomes and reflectors. It'll form the basis of an effective jury rig should the mainmast go over the side – as long as the two are not connected by a triatic stay. It makes a convenient anchoring point for a cockpit awning. And, last but not least, ketches and yawls look good.

No one who saw the breathtaking sight of the big Whitbread maxi ketches of the early 1990s, storming along on five-sail reaches, is likely to forget it in a hurry. Those boats, with their heavily roached mizzens and huge mizzen staysails and asymmetric spinnakers, represented the biggest step forward in ketch development in a generation. Their lead was followed by people like American circumnavigator Steve Dashew, whose big Sundeer ketches with fully-battened mizzens perform very well upwind as well as downwind. You will be hard pressed to find a ketch rig on a boat of less than 40ft – many designers and owners would not consider it in anything under 50ft. Although the ketch rig is now mainly found on big boats, it is far from dead.

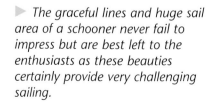 The graceful lines and huge sail area of a schooner never fail to impress but are best left to the enthusiasts as these beauties certainly provide very challenging sailing.

The modern junk rig, its design tried
and tested through the centuries,
has now been so refined that it can
easily be managed by one person.
A poor performer to windward, but
the junk really comes into its own
on a reach or run.

13 Unstayed Rigs

The case for unstayed rigs

A yacht's rig is only as strong as its weakest component, and there is a multiplicity of potentially weak components on any boat. Add up the number of wires, terminals, bottlescrews, tangs, toggles, clevis pins, split pins and spreaders on your boat and then imagine what would happen if any of those parts failed during a rough-weather beat.

Then think about the stresses placed on a hull; the standing rigging is trying to drive the mast down through the deck or the bottom of the hull and at the same time pulling the ends of the boat upwards, while the chainplates want to pull themselves away from the hull and deck. Imagine the forces when your boat flies off the top of a wave and slams into the trough. Phew... with all this to worry about it's a wonder any of us can sleep at night.

These are some of the arguments thrown around in casual conversation by builders and owners of boats with free-standing rigs, and they're hard to dispute. From an engineering viewpoint, the bermudian rig, however well built, is an accident looking for somewhere inconvenient to happen.

Sailpower

A free-standing spar puts no compression forces into the boat's structure; rather than trying to force its way down through the hull, it wants to lift itself out of the boat and has to be secured with a pin through its base. A boat designed for a free-standing spar can be built without regard to the distribution of rig loads through the hull, so it can be made lighter without compromising strength. The loadings from an unstayed mast are lateral, and are placed on the mast partners and surrounding deck area, which must be built up to compensate. Any unstayed mast has to be keel-stepped and the area around the step also needs substantial reinforcement. All other loadings are absorbed by the spar itself, which must be able to bend without breaking. Junk-rigged boats, New England catboats, luggers, sharpies, and the like, traditionally have low aspect-ratio sailplans, with short solid or hollow wood masts, though aluminium is sometimes used. Rigs with high aspect ratios, like those of cat ketches and sloops, need something stronger, and carbon fibre has provided the solution to that problem.

Performance under sail

Even the most evangelical of supporters has to admit that when it comes to windward performance, unstayed rigs are no match for bermudian rigs. There are several reasons for this. The fact that a thick mast section is the first part of the rig to meet the wind is one. Another is the absence of a headsail. A mainsail only does its job as long as the airflow along its lee side remains attached – it will eventually break away into turbulence, and this usually occurs around the point of maximum draft, the deepest part of the sail. After it reaches this point the flow tends to detach and the sail loses drive. The jib deflects air on to the leeward side of the main, keeping the flow attached for longer. Without the jib, the flow breaks away earlier and the main stalls if it's sheeted in too flat, as anyone who's tried to sail a bermudian boat to windward without a jib will know. The turbulence from the mast section compounds this problem.

Sailmakers try to get around this by building the sail so that the maximum draft is further aft, attempting to trick the flow into staying attached for longer. With the draft so far aft a large amount of sideways thrust is generated and to counteract that, the main must be eased further when going to windward than would be the case if the boat had a jib.

The same rules of trim apply to big una-rigged (single sail) boats and cat ketches; they generally need to be sailed a little free, especially in light airs. Designers have tried various ways of improving the windward bite of these rigs, including rotating, aerodynamically-shaped masts, but without a slot there is only so much that can be done. It is interesting to note that Freedom Yachts resorted to putting forestays on their newer cruising designs purely so jibs could be carried; the inevitable sag in the unsupported jib luff was to some extent countered by building a semi-rigid horizontal batten into the headsail.

Another reason for the indifferent windward performance of most boats of this type relates to hull type and design. If a mast is stepped in the bows the hull needs to be quite full forward to carry the weight,

▲ *The cat ketch is a powerful and, in its own way, attractive rig.*

and full bows are not usually associated with good windward ability. An exception to this rule is the Wyliecat range from California, whose designer, Tom Wylie, has placed carbon fibre cat rigs into performance-orientated hulls with good results; owners of these boats, the largest of which is 48ft, report good pointing ability and a fine turn of speed on all points of sail except downwind in light airs. Wylie designed the cat-rigged Open 60 *Ocean Planet* which was entered in the 2002/3 Around Alone race. As a rule, though, cat ketch and junk rigs are usually put into moderately heavy displacement hulls which are designed more for good seakeeping than windward work.

Where unstayed rigs really score is in offwind sailing. On a reach or a run, catboats, junk-rigged boats and cat ketches will really steam along in any sort of a breeze. Reaching is especially good fun on a cat ketch. You effectively have two mainsails driving the boat, both trimmed for maximum aerodynamic efficiency; compare this to a conventional rig where the headsail will lose its shape, and therefore much of its drive, once eased out past a beam reach. There is no need to worry about chafe, because there are no shrouds for the sail to bear up against. Because the foresail is effectively poled out to leeward you can sail at deeper angles before it is blanketed by the main. A cat ketch rig on a good hull will comfortably outrun similar-sized bermudian sloops or ketches in sustained reaching conditions, and place little stress on her crew.

Free-standing rigs are good in heavy weather too. The spars bend in puffs, automatically flattening and depowering the sails as well as spilling the wind. The boat will not heel as much and will make less leeway. Beating in a seaway, the masts will flex and absorb the shock loadings from punching into head seas. (This same characteristic works against them when they're motoring into a sharp sea with no sail up – the mast(s) whip around annoyingly).

You don't see many una-rigged cruising boats longer than around 35 feet, simply because the mainsail gets increasingly harder for a small crew to handle. A boat also needs a lot of initial stability if it is to carry just one large sail, as demonstrated by the extreme beaminess of most catboats. A side effect of this beaminess coupled with shallow draught is an unpleasant motion in a seaway, so catboats are at their best in sheltered waters. For bigger boats, especially if they are to go offshore, the rig generally needs to be split into more manageable proportions.

The Freedom revolution

There are drawings of cat ketches, a hybrid between a schooner and a ketch with one mast in the bows and the other close to amidships, going back to the 16th century. In the 1920s, the American designer L Francis Herreshoff was experimenting with two and three-masted unstayed rigs carrying wishbone booms and no headsails. As the saying goes, there's nothing new under the sun. But it wasn't until the 1970s that the cat ketch came of age, when the visionary American Garry Hoyt combined wishbone booms with two-ply sails that wrapped around the free-standing spars to create a blunt aerofoil and minimise mast turbulence. He

Sailpower

The carbon fibre mast of the Freedom 30 adds strength, and its lighter weight and lack of heavy rigging wires lowers the centre of gravity and makes for a stiffer boat.

placed this rig into the Freedom 33 hull designed by Jay Paris, and that design was the progenitor of the most common type of freestanding rig in use today.

After some spectacular early failures, the aluminium spars of the early Freedoms were replaced with carbon fibre. Carbon fibre is perfect for freestanding masts, being lighter than aluminium or wood and considerably stronger. A smaller section can be used, which decreases disturbance to the sail's luff when going to windward. The light weight, combined with the absence of heavy rigging wires, lowers the centre of gravity and makes for a stiffer boat. As carbon fibre technology has improved over the years, failure has become rare but not unheard of, though when the cat ketch ocean racer *Lady Pepperell* was pitchpoled in the Southern Ocean she came upright with both masts standing and silenced a fair few critics. Long-distance cruisers are right to be wary of the material, for if it should fail in some remote place, repair would be almost impossible.

On the Freedom cat ketch, the wishbone is attached to the mast some way above the sail's tack. It is angled down towards the sail's clew and acts as a vang or kicking strap to prevent the sail from twisting excessively. Its arms are curved to stop them from chafing the sail. This is quite an efficient setup, because the draft in the sail is easy to control by means of the clew outhauls, while the vanging influence means the sail keeps a constant shape when eased out.

The lack of shrouds allows the booms to swing forward of the mast so you can sail by the lee quite happily, and if you goose-wing the sails square to the masts you have a powerful, well-balanced downwind rig, with the option of using a mizzen staysail in light airs; it is the latter practice that has led to most of the spar failures on cat ketches, though.

To windward, it is a different story. The mizzen operates in the dirty air from the foresail and with no headsail to provide a slot, the cat ketch will not point as high as a bermudian sloop. The difference is most noticeable in light airs and how much it matters depends on where and how you sail.

Free-standing masts don't usually carry forestays because without a backstay there is no means of keeping the luff of the jib tight, and the pressure from the headsail bends the mast the wrong way, also spoiling the mainsail shape. However, it did not take the performance-minded Hoyt long before he developed the 'cat sloop', with a single mast and a forestay whose sole purpose is to carry a jib for improved windward performance, as seen on newer Freedoms like the 35 and 45. The jib has a floppy batten to provide luff tension.

Over the last decade or so, the cat ketch concept in general has undergone some refinements. In many cases the sails now run on tracks rather than sleeving around the spar and have fully-battened sails with conventional booms. The extra roach permitted by the absence of backstays gives the sail a more efficient wing-like shape which improves light-airs performance. US designer Eric Sponberg, one of the greatest advocates of free-standing rigs, has developed a rotating carbon spar system which is said to noticeably improve performance.

AeroRig

The principle of a rotating rig goes back long before Ian Howlett designed the AeroRig and Carbospars started to produce it. German sailor Carl Boss developed the concept in the early 1970s as a response to the downwind inefficiency of the bermudian rig, and in the 1980s it enjoyed some popularity with French Open class multihull racers. It remained on the outskirts until the early 1990s; since then, Carbospars has fitted more than a hundred to monohulls and multihulls of all descriptions.

The AeroRig is great for those who like their sailing to be uncomplicated. Its unstayed carbon fibre mast and GRP boom carry a conventional main/jib combination. The whole lot revolves to present the sails at the optimum angle to the wind, so in effect the sails are always trimmed for a beat whenever the wind is on or forward of the beam. In fact you don't really need to touch them at all once they're hoisted and trimmed for the wind conditions – slightly eased for light airs, flatter for strong winds – whatever point of sail you're on, because the rig thinks it's always beating.

If you let go of the mainsheet, the rig will point into the wind and weathercock gently. Gybing is wonderfully quiet and stress-free. You don't even need to touch a sheet – just bear away until the main swings across the boat. As this happens the jib is heading in the opposite direction and backwinds in time to take the sting out of the gybe. Running, the sailplan is squared off across the boat and the boom can be eased well forward of 90 degrees. There are no winches in the cockpit.

Sailpower

Like any rig, the AeroRig is not without its faults. The jib luff tends to sag when beating in a breeze and there is no way of tensioning it. Sail controls are on the boom, so you need to go to the mast to reef. While a conventional sloop can continue sailing under headsail while the main is being reefed, on the AeroRig boat the jib has to be rolled away first. In-boom furling has been widely adopted by AeroRig owners, making the reefing process fast and easy.

Its main drawback is expense – several times the cost of a conventional aluminium rig. A few years ago I took part in a test between an AeroRig versus a conventional sloop rig on two identical hulls. Unsurprisingly, the AeroRig excelled downwind, while the conventional sloop had the edge on a beat.

There have been other variations on the principle epitomised by the AeroRig, though none have met with the same commercial success. Garry Hoyt has recently developed his own version, and it will be interesting to see if any manufacturers put it into production

The junk

If longevity is a measure of an idea's worth then the junk is about the most worthy rig around; it dates back to Roman times. It has only relatively recently been adopted by cruising yachtsmen, though more than a century ago no less a sailor than Joshua Slocum pronounced it the handiest small-boat rig in the world.

The man who adapted the Chinese rig for cruising purposes was Colonel 'Blondie' Hasler, who fitted a junk sail to his Folkboat, *Jester*, in 1959. A year later he sailed her to second place in the first single-handed transatlantic race, establishing the rig's credentials to sceptical Westerners.

The 'modern' junk rig as developed by Hasler has an indisputably Chinese look to it but has been refined so that it can be operated by one person without the need to go on deck or handle the sail(s). So easy is it to work that Mike Richey, who took over *Jester* from Hasler, was still crossing oceans singlehanded in her when well into his eighties. The sail, with all its battens, is heavy and can be a handful to hoist but is the simplest of any to reef; just ease the halyard and the sail will rattle down under its own weight to lie quietly in its lazyjacks. Sail can be shortened panel by panel.

It is a quiet rig, with the full-length battens eliminating flogging and no shrouds for the wind to howl through, and because the sail extends forward of the mast it is semi-balanced, making gybing an innocuous affair, even in a breeze.

Aerodynamically, the junk sail is at a disadvantage in light airs because its battens are designed to keep it flat at all times, and there is no way of controlling draft. In more of a breeze, the flat sail comes into its own, providing drive without excessive heeling. In general, junk-rigged boats do not go to windward at all well in light airs. It's a different story on a reach or a run. On a reach, the multiple sheets allow each panel to be adjusted individually to control or induce twist, and on a run the entire sail area can be presented square to the wind.

Light airs running is another weak point, for there is no safe way of increasing downwind sail area. The sail is hard to trim, because it does not tell you when it is not at the optimum angle to the wind, so telltales are important. On balance though, the junk rig's benefits far outweigh its disadvantages when it comes to shorthanded long-distance cruising. Not least of these is that it is cheap to build and maintain.

The eye of the beholder

Given all these arguments one would expect to see unstayed rigs everywhere, yet the sight of one in open waters is a relatively unusual occurrence. Devotees of free-standing rigs still find themselves elbowed into the fringes of the pleasure-sailing population, striving to make their voices heard.

The reasons are simple enough. Yachtsmen are, by and large, a pretty conservative bunch who find it difficult to trust a spar not held upright by copious amounts of wire. Nor can the importance of aesthetics be understated. Catboats and cat ketches look ungainly and unbalanced to eyes brought up on bermudian rigs, and junks, well, junk rigs look outlandish. It is no coincidence that the only free-standing rig to have won widespread approval in recent years, the AeroRig, is essentially an unstayed bermudian rig.

Nevertheless, the stayed bermudian rig has just about reached the end of its evolutionary road and, with the amount of development going into free-standing rigs, we'll be seeing a lot more of them in the future. French design house Groupe Finot is keen to see more of its Open 60 designs with unstayed or semi-stayed carbon fibre wingmast rigs, which it claims are much more efficient for shorthanded sailing and ultimately for cruising.

◄ *Blondie Hasler's famous Folkboat,* Jester, *proved the junk rig's worth with multiple ocean crossings.* Photo *courtesy of* Yachting Monthly.

14 Easy Upgrades

The traveller

Genoa cars

Backstay tensioner

The kicking strap

Winches

Better blocks

Theorising about sail trim is all very well but when it comes time to practise what the experts preach, many cruisers will find their boats working against them instead of with them. Sail handling and trimming systems, as well as the way decks and cockpits are laid out, are always a compromise, and builders will often lavish less attention to these vital factors than to accommodation and styling.

Because they are built to a price, most production boats leave the factory equipped with undersized winches and the most basic of sail trimming gear. Except in rare cases it will all work, but equally, it's a rare boat that won't benefit from having a bit of time and, yes, money lavished on unglamorous but important items like mainsheet tackles and travellers, kickers, backstay tensioners and halyards.

Upgrading deck gear to make sail handling and trim easier will enhance your sailing life. The more difficult it is to change a sheet lead, harden up the kicker or winch the genoa in for that vital last couple of inches, the more likely it is that people simply won't bother. Consequently the sails will seldom be trimmed properly and the boat won't be sailing to her potential.

The traveller

The mainsheet traveller is an important trimming control and when the wind is forward of the beam it usually needs adjusting for each change in wind speed and direction, so a user-friendly, low-friction system should be high on the shopping list.

Loads on traveller cars can be very high, especially on the mainsail-driven fractionally-rigged boats that became popular during the 1990s. In a stiff breeze, the last thing you want to do is to wrestle with sticky plunger stops, risking your fingertips to get a binding traveller car down to leeward, then manually heaving it up to weather again. This gets so wearying that many people simply don't bother to use the traveller.

Replacing the traveller is an easy upgrade, especially on older boats where the track runs across the bridgedeck or the transom. Most deck gear makers now offer traveller cars that run on recirculating ball bearings, cutting friction to a minimum, and can be hauled up to weather via a pulley system. These make a huge difference to any boat. Depending on mainsail area, a 2:1 purchase should be adequate for boats up to 35ft.

If your T-track is so old that modern traveller cars aren't suitable, you will have to replace that too. Replacing the track is not the nightmare it once was; Lewmar and others can supply 'sliding bolt' track, which has captive bolts that slide back and forth until they line up perfectly with the holes in the deck.

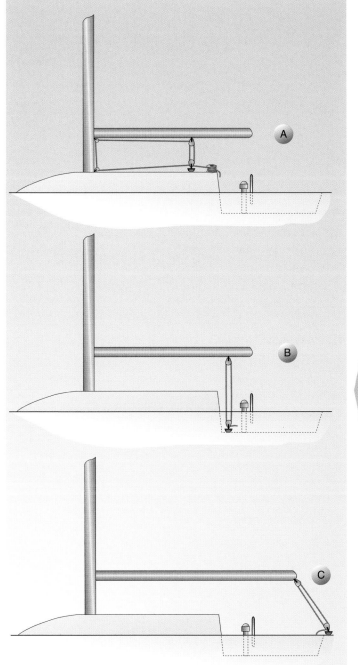

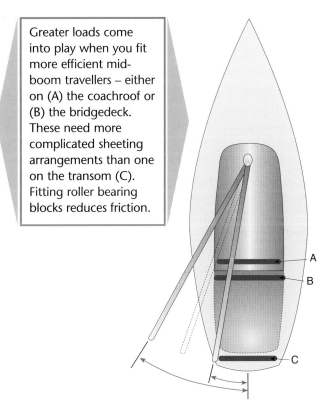

Greater loads come into play when you fit more efficient mid-boom travellers – either on (A) the coachroof or (B) the bridgedeck. These need more complicated sheeting arrangements than one on the transom (C). Fitting roller bearing blocks reduces friction.

Sailpower

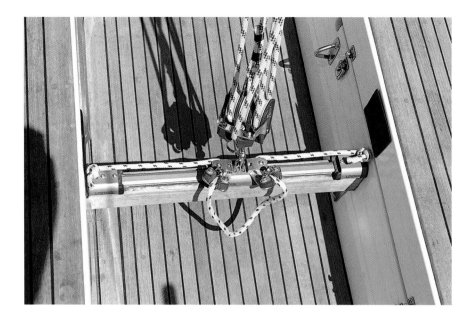

◄ *Adding a mainsheet traveller will increase your trimming options.*

▼ *An adjustable genoa car gives you the ability to handle the sheet leads easily and quickly.*

Genoa cars

Does the following scenario ring a bell? You've just taken a few rolls in the genoa, and now the sheet lead is wrong; the sail is luffing at the top and the foot is stretched tight. You have two choices. You can ignore it, and carry on regardless with a poorly trimmed sail, or you can send a person forward along the lee deck to move the car forward while the sheet bashes him around the ears. After a while, scarcely anyone seems to bother, and the genoa cars may as well be welded in place for all the attention they get.

This is why fitting towable genoa cars can change your sailing life. If you have the ability to adjust the sheet leads easily and quickly without having to leave the cockpit, then you are going to do it; it becomes a pleasure instead of a chore.

Lewmar, Harken and other deck gear makers all offer towable genoa cars that run on bearings or low-friction composite slides. With sliding bolt track, they make an easy do-it-yourself upgrade that inceases performance at the expense of a little more line in the cockpit. Most people consider this a fair trade. A 2:1 purchase is ample for most boats up to 45 feet, but sheeting angles need to be taken into account when working out the specifications for the cars; the more vertical the sheet lead between car and clew, the higher the loading on the car, and the more force will be required to tow it forward.

Backstay tensioner

Every fractionally-rigged boat will have (or should have) a means of adjusting backstay tension. Its main purpose is to flatten and depower the mainsail in stronger winds, putting off the time at which a reef will be required, and they don't have much effect on forestay tension, which is controlled by the cap shrouds. Because very few masthead-rigged boats are provided with backstay adjusters, cruising sailors regard them with the deepest suspicion – 'just another thing to go wrong'. But on a masthead rig, backstay tension determines how much tension there is in the forestay, and therefore how well the genoa sets. In light winds, ease the backstay for a fuller, more powerful genoa; in stronger winds, tension the backstay to get the draft out of the genoa and improve the boat's pointing ability and balance. Few production boats have backstay tensioners fitted as standard, because of the cost, and because builders are worried that owners who do not know what they are doing would misuse the devises and damage the boat or rig.

Fitting a backstay tensioner need not be an expensive process, depending on the backstay arrangement. Masthead-rigged boats over 35 feet or so, with single backstays taken to a chain plate mounted centrally at the transom, will require a hydraulic or mechanical adjuster.

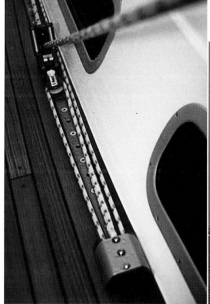

▲ Towable genoa cars reduce friction and improve efficiency.

▶ Only racing boats used to have adjustable backstays, but some cruisers have now followed suit.

Sailpower

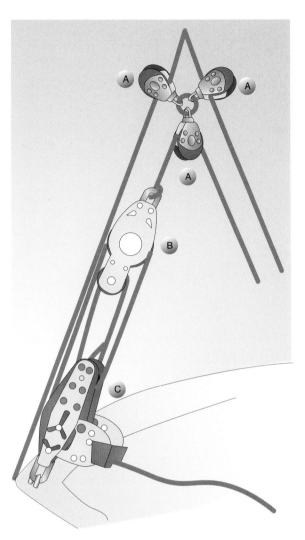

Two approaches to adding backstay tensioners; above, a common 'pinch' arrangement for a partially split backstay.
Below, this tackle acts on the two parts of a double-backstay setup. It looks as though it would need to be taken to a winch.

Mechanical adjusters are operated either by winch handle, wheels or flip-up handles and they're simple and sturdy but they're also slow to operate. A typical self-contained hydraulic backstay adjuster like those made by Navtec is quick and easy to adjust, and usually has the advantage of a relief valve which will prevent the adjuster from overloading the rig. Both types of adjuster should have a scale or gauge fitted so that the optimum settings can be noted and repeated. Backstay adjusters should be fitted by professional riggers, as the penalties for poor installation can be severe.

On fractionally-rigged (and some masthead-rigged) boats you will often see split backstays, with chainplates on the quarters. Usually, the twin backstays are joined to a single wire two or three metres up from the deck like an inverted Y. Replacing the tang with a sheave and one arm of the Y with a block and tackle is an easy and cost-effective process. The sheave must be large in diameter and the tackle purchase should be 6:1, with good-quality, low-friction triple blocks. Measure it carefully, because it will probably need to be longer than you think: up to a metre at full extension. A wire or Spectra strop should be fitted between the backstay and the chainplate as a failsafe to ensure the mast won't fall down if the tackle breaks or is accidentally released.

Another common method on boats under 30ft is to rig a pincher tackle – a block on each arm of the Y attached to a 6:1 downhaul,

Most cruising boats have inadequate or non-existent backstay tensioners. To bend the mast and flatten the mainsail (fractional rig) or tension a sagging forestay (masthead rig), a powerful backstay adjuster is essential. This system has a triple-block setup (A) operating on a split backstay. To get enough power, a 4:1 tackle (B) has been fitted, led through the lower block (C) down to the chain plate. This cascade system doubles the purchase. Tackle adjusters are only suitable for boats smaller than around 33 feet (10m), above that you need a mechanical or hydraulic adjuster.

which draws the two together, thereby tensioning the backstay. These offer great purchase at light loads but it decreases as the wires are drawn closer together; the longer the legs of the Y, and the closer together they are to begin with, the more efficient the tackle.

The kicking strap

A kicking strap (boom vang) is essential on any boat to control mainsail shape after the limits of the traveller have been reached. Without a kicker, the main boom will lift as the mainsheet is eased and the top of the sail will twist off to leeward, spilling the wind. Inexperienced sailors will then tend to sheet in the main until the top of the sail stops luffing, with the result that the lower part of the main will be overtrimmed; this is certain to cause excess weather helm and a consequent reduction in boat speed.

If you are sailing downwind with the mainsail eased right out, the top of the sail can twist so far off that it is forward of the shrouds. This encourages the boat's tendency to roll and can lead to a nasty broach. Tensioning the kicker so that the twist is eliminated will stabilise the sail and decrease the rolling.

On a reach, if the wind pipes up to the extent that the boat is on the verge of becoming overpressed and weather helm is becoming more apparent, then easing the kicker to induce some twist in the sail and open the upper part off the leech will relieve the heeling forces and take some of the weight off the helm.

Although the kicker doesn't need to be adjustable over a range of more than a few inches, it does need to be very powerful. By virtue of its location in the forward part of the boom, there is about twice as much loading on the kicker as there is on the mainsheet. On some boats the kicker can be used in conjunction with the backstay to bend the mast, flatten the mainsail and take some of the loading off the mainsheet when going to windward.

A decent kicking strap or boom vang helps to flatten the sail and prevent twist when you ease the mainsheet.

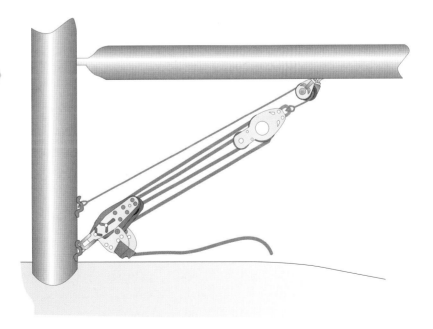

Sailpower

Generally, the kicker is not used when going to windward because the mainsheet applies enough tension on the mainsail leech, and the sail's angle of attack is controlled by playing the traveller. Many smaller, usually fractionally-rigged boats do not have travellers, though, and so a powerful, well set-up kicker is even more important.

Since the kicker is so important, it is strange that so many boats sport weedy assemblies of undersized blocks and poor-quality, stretchy line. The blocks on the kicking strap system should be at least the same size as those on the mainsheet tackle. The purchase should be at least 6:1, but more won't hurt; on boats above 40ft, a 12:1 purchase, achieved by using a cascade system of multiple tackles, is not unusual.

Upgrading to a more efficient block and tackle system incorporating low-friction ball bearing blocks is not prohibitively expensive. Most people, though, upgrade to a gas or spring-loaded kicker which has the advantage of supporting the boom, thereby allowing the topping lift to be dispensed with.

Many sailors – and all sailmakers – detest the topping lift because it swings around and chafes on the proud seams of the sail. You should think twice before getting rid of it if you are contemplating long offshore passages. If its sheave is strong enough, the topping lift can make a good backup for the main halyard.

▶ *A sheet winch should be positioned so you can crouch over it and swing a 10in handle.*

Winches

The sheer cost of sheet winches means they're usually not even considered when the boat's systems are being upgraded, except when the decision is made to go to self-tailing winches. Even then, most people opt for the same size. Winches are expensive, but choosing not to upgrade can be a false economy. Most boatbuilders fit the smallest winches they can get away with, in order to help keep the overall boat cost down. If, according to the maker's winch selection guide, the boat length or headsail size is in the upper range for, say, a number 40 and the lower range for a 44, the builder will fit a 40 every time.

Consequently, while the headsail might be easy to trim while eating into a balmy force 3, an extra five knots of wind can have the poor trimmer croaking pathetically for a luff. A person with plenty of upper body strength will cope but weaker members of the crew will struggle. Tiredness, seasickness, and the difficulty of working in rough conditions are also situations where many crew will wish for more powerful winches.

A winch operates on a simple principle. Force is applied via the winch handle and transmitted to the drum via reduction gears which increase power by reducing the speed of rotation. The final power ratio is usually indicated by the name of the winch, ie a 44 has a power ratio of 44:1. In theory, it generates 48 kilos of power for every kilo put into it through the winch handle.

Winch makers base their calculations on the assumption that a normal adult can exert a load of around 25 kilos (55lb) on a winch through a standard 10in winch handle. Multiplied by the winch's power ratio, this is the factor limiting the load which the trimmer can

▲ *Electric self-tailing sheet winches can take much of the effort out of sail handling.*

handle. Thus a number 40 winch, with its power ratio of 40:1, would have a theoretical pulling power of approximately 1000kg (2200lb) while a number 44 winch pulls around 1100kg (2420lb).

These calculations are optimistic, especially in the context of family sailing. Weaker crew will not be able to put anywhere near 25kg of load on the winch, especially in a breeze; 10-15kg will be more realistic. Internal friction can also sap as much as 40 per cent of a winch's power in low gear. Add the friction loss from turning blocks and that 40:1 power ratio doesn't look so generous any more; you'll be lucky to get half the rated pull of the winch. All this adds up to the inescapable conclusion that when it comes to winches, bigger is definitely better. The ultimate winch upgrade is to hydraulically or electrically powered units and these are becoming popular even on quite small boats.

Location, location, location

A winch's efficiency is also affected by its location. Some builders seem to go to a lot of trouble to make their winches as hard to use as possible. There should be room to crouch over the winch and swing a 10in handle without it fouling the guardrails or sprayhood fittings. Most winches are located on cockpit coamings, which can be a good or bad thing depending on the shape of the coaming and its relationship to the seat. Generally, the further inboard the winch can be located, the easier it will be to operate. On some newer boats with genoa tracks on the coachroof sides, the sheet winches are also mounted on the coachroof, which is not a bad place as long as the winch handles do not foul the sprayhood.

Many winches are angled outboard to ensure a good lead from the sheet cars; this can make them difficult to operate at high angles of heel. On a late-model production boat, with winch plinths moulded into place, you are usually stuck with what you have. Older boats may well offer more scope for altering the position of a primary winch.

The angle at which the line enters the drum is critical. Too shallow or too steep, and the line will form riding turns on the drum. The optimum angle is between 5 and 8 degrees.

Handles

If bigger winches are out of the question, a longer winch handle will make a surprising difference to the power the average person can apply to a winch. The 10in winch handle is the industry standard because it is a comfortable size for most people to use. Replacing a 10in handle with a 12in handle will increase leverage by 20 per cent at the cost of an increased swinging circle; conversely, while an 8in handle will allow to you to grind a lot faster, its leverage drops by 20 per cent. Still, in light airs where is not a lot of force on the sails, an 8in handle will help you get the sail trimmed a lot faster. A double-handed 10in winch handle is a good investment, letting you use much more upper-body strength.

WIND

The weight of wind in a sail increases as the square of the wind strength. The formula to calculate wind pressure in the sail is $F=0.00431 \times A \times V^2$; F is the weight in the sail in pounds, A is the sail area in square feet and V is the windspeed in knots.

This formula doesn't take into account the increase in the force required to winch in the sail caused by sheeting angle and point of sail. The more vertical the sheet lead, the greater the force required; the closer the yacht is sailing to the wind, the more weight there is in the sail.

▲ *Bigger winches are an expensive upgrade, but they will improve the quality of your sailing life.*

▲ *A clutch like this secures a line under load and means that you can use a winch for more than one purpose.*

Clutches

Decent rope clutches, as opposed to jammers, can make a lot of difference to line handling. A clutch will release a line under load, while a jammer needs to have the load taken up on a winch before it can be released.

It's especially worthwhile leading the kicking strap to a clutch. The loads on a kicker are twice as high as those on the mainsheet and often it's impossible to get the required amount of tension without leading it via a winch to a rope clutch.

Modern rope clutches are, all in all, good pieces of kit, but have their own peculiarities. They're sensitive to line size, and line type. Many cheap ropes aren't the diameter they're supposed to be. Often what's sold as a 12mm rope turns out to be 13mm, and that's when you get them sticking in the clutches. Cheap ropes also stretch more under load, making them more likely to slip through the clutch.

Better blocks

Friction is the sail trimmer's enemy. Every time a moving rope passes around a sheave some power is lost and whoever is hauling on that line has to work harder to make up for it.

When a block is heavily loaded, 10 per cent or more of the force is lost to friction, depending on the efficiency of the sheave's bearing or bushing. This can mean that to pull a 100lb load you'd need to exert a force of 110lb, and each sheave in the system adds a little more friction. Ball or roller bearing blocks can cut this loss to 2 per cent.

Back in the days of natural fibre ropes there was a rule of thumb that the sheave diameter should be at least five times that of the line. The greater flexibility and smoothness of manmade fibre ropes means that is no longer a hard and fast rule. The bigger the block, the better; but as importantly, the rope should be sized correctly so that it is not too big for the groove in the sheave.

The lead to turning blocks and sheaves is also important. Lines should be led evenly and fairly to all blocks to minimise friction. If a highly-loaded line enters or leaves a sheave at an angle, then the stress on the block will be very high and could well cause it to fail.

How the load on sheaves changes according to the lead of the line. This has a bearing on friction and general efficiency.

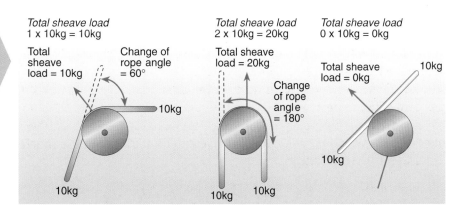

Total sheave load
1 x 10kg = 10kg

Total sheave load = 10kg
Change of rope angle = 60°
10kg
10kg

Total sheave load
2 x 10kg = 20kg

Total sheave load = 20kg
Change of rope angle = 180°
10kg 10kg

Total sheave load
0 x 10kg = 0kg

Total sheave load = 0kg
10kg
10kg

Sailpower

The chances are that the blocks on your boat will be the smallest the builder could get away with using. Replacing them with bigger versions, even if not the ball-bearing type, will cut friction and loadings. This is particularly important with footblocks which are used to lead genoa sheets to the winch; a return angle approaching 180 degrees, as is often seen, puts nearly twice as much strain on the block as is on the sheet. You wouldn't want to be in the way if the block let go. As a guide, lines that need frequent adjustment while under a load will benefit from ball or roller-bearing blocks. These include genoa sheets and furling line, the mainsheet, traveller, and kicking strap.

On many yachts you'll find the genoa furling line led back to the quarter and turned 180 degrees through an undersized block to lead to a spinnaker winch. If the block was properly sized – that means at least a 30mm sheave for a 6mm line – and located further forward so that the line leads to the cockpit at an angle of 45 degrees or less, the genoa would be much easier to furl by hand.

▼ *Simple furling line leads are easy to fit and, correctly positioned, can make it easier to roll up a genoa.*

▲ *Modern roller-bearing blocks reduce friction.*

▶ This furling line lead is fine until it exits the clutch; the angle to the block will noticeably increase friction.

Purchase power

The block and tackle has been the sailor's best friend since the age of the Greeks. Along with the winch and its reduction gears it is the easiest and simplest way of mechanically increasing the strength of a human being. The mechanical advantage of a tackle is determined by the number of 'parts' or lengths of line between the blocks. If the tackle has four parts, then the energy that is put into it is increased fourfold; a 10kg pull on the tail will move a 40kg load. The more parts in the tackle, the greater the mechanical advantage.

The simplest way to improve the efficiency of mainsheet and kicker set-ups is to increase the purchase of their tackles. For instance, upgrading the mainsheet tackle from 4:1 to 6:1 means 30 per cent less effort is needed to harden the sheet in when the wind pipes up. The other side of the coin is that the greater the purchase, the slower the speed at which it can be operated. A 4:1 purchase means pulling through 4 inches of line to move shorten the tackle by one inch. On a 6:1 tackle, you will need to haul in six inches of line to shorten the tackle by one inch. Another factor to consider is that increasing the purchase means adding more blocks, and therefore more friction, into the system.

Why it is so important to have low-friction blocks in a mainsheet system – the loads increase each time the line passes through a right angle in a sheave, and the load on the first block is doubled.

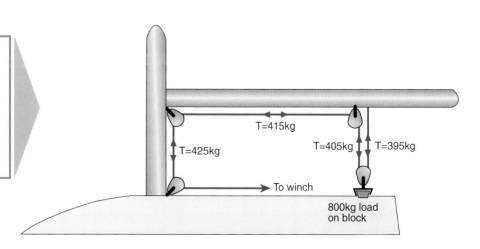

T=415kg

T=425kg

T=405kg   T=395kg

To winch

800kg load on block

15
Running Rigging

What rope?

Rope construction

The right rope for the job

▽ *With so many different kinds of rope on the market it is vital to get the right one for the job.*

Why are there so many kinds of rope? Because there are so many different jobs for it to do. If you took this to its extreme, you'd have a different line for almost every application. There's no need to go that far, although some do. Far more common is using just one rope throughout the boat, and that's not ideal either. There is no simple answer; it depends on your budget, and how important good performance is to you. One thing is for sure, and that is that shoddy halyards and sheets make sailing a boat harder work and, ultimately, a less satisfying experience.

Apart from a few dyed-in-the-wool traditionalists, who run very old boats and refuse to have them sullied by modern materials, you'd have to be a member of the Flat Earth Society to favour natural fibre ropes over modern synthetics. If Joshua Slocum had been offered a couple of reels of pre-stretched polyester you can bet he'd have ditched his manila and hemp sheets and halyards before you could say circumnavigate.

Natural fibre ropes are unpredictable in quality, prone to rot, stretch and break at inconvenient moments, and uncomfortable to handle; small wonder yachtsmen cast them aside without a second thought once a viable alternative arrived.

What rope?

We now have a choice of materials and constructions that is as confusing as it is varied. What makes some types better for certain jobs than others? Why can't one rope perform every function on a boat? Are the latest superfibres any use for cruising ropes? To be able to answer questions like these it helps to understand the properties of different fibres.

Polyester

Rope made from this princely fibre, more commonly known as Dacron or Terylene, can be used for virtually any application on a boat, from mooring warps to halyards. The exception is anchor warp, where nylon's greater stretch gives it superior shock-absorbing properties. Low stretch, high strength, long life, good resistance to chafe, chemicals and ultraviolet light; polyester has it all. It's also pleasant to handle. Two varieties are used in ropemaking: *spun polyester*, in which the yarns are spun from short fibres, making the rope fuzzy, and *filament*, where the yarns are made up of continuous fibres. The latter is more slippery but stronger and not as stretchy.

Polypropylene

This comes in many varieties – *multifilament, monofilament, spun, three-strand, plaited* – all of which float. Polypropylene has traditionally had poor UV resistance, although modern ropes will have UV inhibitors added to the fibres. The most common polypropylene rope is the ubiquitous blue stuff which, discarded by fishermen, floats around the coast waiting for a propeller to wrap itself around. Most of the major marine rope makers now produce braided polypropylene rope which, to look at, is almost identical to polyester; it can be used for sheets on dinghies or small budget cruisers but is nowhere near as strong as polyester and stretches more too.

Dyneema

Known as Spectra in the US, this is more accurately if prosaically called HMPE, High Modulus Polyethylene. It has a very high strength to weight ratio and is much more versatile than Kevlar. Aside from its minimal stretch, it doesn't mind being knotted or forced around tight corners and so can be used for sheets and sail control lines as well as halyards. Its resistance to chafe and UV light means it can be stripped of its polyester cover for even more weight saving; not that cruisers will want to go that far. It is very expensive.

Kevlar

Not so long ago, this aramid fibre was the rope to have – on a top-flight racing boat. Extremely strong, with amazingly low stretch, it's used as a core on halyards, spinnaker guys and other lines where minimal stretch is desirable. It's also expensive, degrades if the core is exposed to sunlight, and is not very durable; it wears out quickly when continually forced around a tight radius, ie a block. Hence the large amounts of Kevlar found in skips around Hamble marinas after an Admiral's Cup week.

Vectran

This is a liquid crystal polymer fibre, even stronger and less stretchy than Dyneema and even more expensive. Its UV resistance is not quite as good and nor is its abrasion resistance. It does however have very good fatigue characteristics.

PBO

This is the newest high-tech fibre, and is the strongest of the lot. It can be damaged by common chemicals and and its UV resistance is poor. Like Vectran and Dyneema, it needs to be sheathed in a polyester cover. Increasingly being used for standing rigging in top-end racing boats, it is exceedingly expensive, about 35 times the cost of polyester.

Rope construction

Most manmade fibres are polymers – that is, they are derived from oil by a chemical process called polymerisation, which forms a long molecular chain. To cut a very long story short, chemists tweak, tune and fiddle about with these chains until they arrive at the desired characteristics for the fibre – strength, stretch resistance, and so on. No matter what fibre is involved, the manufacturing process is the same. Very fine filaments are twisted into a yarn, yarns are twisted together into a final yarn, the final yarns are twisted into strands or plaits, and the strands or

▲ Dyneema is the most expensive low-stretch rope; sometimes it comes with an outer core of polyester (right) to bulk out the rope.

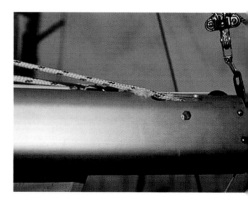

▼ Having chosen the right rope for the job, don't forget to watch out for chafe.

plaits are woven into a rope. Each step in the process involves twisting the yarn in the opposite direction to the previous step, to make sure the rope is balanced. Finally, the rope is heat treated to minimise shrinking and hardening.

This is an oversimplification, and there are many subtleties in the process; suffice to say that the difference between good and poor ropes is more often down to the manufacture than the quality of the fibres.

Three-strand

Of the constructions used for yachting ropes, good old *three-strand* has been around for thousands of years, and until a couple of decades ago, it was in almost universal use for yacht sheets and halyards. It still does good service on plenty of boats; gaffers, for instance, look silly with brightly coloured braided running rigging and so you're more likely to find three-strand in use on traditional craft. Even pre-stretched, its stretch charactics are inferior to braided rope but on traditional boats a little give in the rope is no bad thing. It's also tough, chafe-resistant and dead easy to splice.

Braided

With an inner core covered by an outer sheath of the same material, braided ropes have superseded three-strand for most uses on a boat because of their lower stretch, user-friendliness and greater strength. Cores can be plaited, three-strand or, strongest of all, made of bundles of parallel, continuous filaments. The terms 8-plait and 16-plait simply refer to the number of plaits in the cover, not the core, and there are many variations on these themes depending on whether the rope is to have a floppy or firm feel. Typically, 8-plait, the simplest construction, is used on ropes up to 8mm in diameter, 16 plait for thicker ropes. Braided rope is costlier than three-strand but is a lot more winch-friendly. It doesn't kink and is soft and easy to handle.

Composite

Composite ropes have a core of one fibre and a sheath made from another. Sometimes more than one fibre is used in the core and some will have a double core, or an inner sheath. All the high-tech ropes will have polyester covers to protect the cores, whereas in polyester ropes the cover provides a significant part of ther strength.

All rope, even the expensive exotics, will stretch a little until broken in. The weave relaxes when there is no load on it and it needs to be used a few times before it 'settles'.

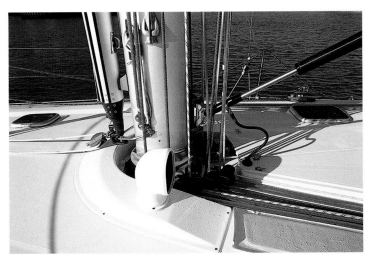

▲ *High-performance cruisers like this Starlight 46 put high loads on their lines and benefit from exotic fibres.*

Sailpower

THE RIGHT ROPE FOR THE JOB

Halyards

How important is stretch? For the sailor who likes to get the best out of the boat, there's nothing more annoying than having to adjust the main halyard continually as the load on it changes and upsets the trim. For the crew of an elderly bilge keeler, stretch might not be an issue at all, because after all they are only cruising, not racing; it should be, though, because it's a shame to have the boat performing below its potential.

Not that long ago, a wire halyard with a rope tail was the only low-stretch option. It's still a serviceable compromise, but it's untidy; if wire jumps a masthead sheave, it will mess up the mast cap. Unless there are a couple of turns of wire around the winch, there is an awfully high loading on the splice. When the wire starts to strand, as it inevitably will, it forms 'meat hooks' which tear up your hands and wreck your sails.

If the time has come to replace a wire/rope halyard, Dyneema/Spectra is the priciest but lowest-stretch option; typically, you can go down a third in rope size from a double braid construction. If the boat has high-tech, low-stretch sails, it will need high-tech halyards. Otherwise, for the average cruising yacht, the extra cost is hard to justify.

For most purposes, a top quality double braided polyester rope will be almost as effective and a whole lot cheaper. By way of comparison, English Braids quotes its Dyneemabraid as stretching 2 per cent at 50 per cent of breaking load; for its braid-on-braid polyester, the stretch at the same percentage of breaking load is 5 per cent. Taken over a halyard length of 40 or 50ft, this could mean 2ft or more of stretch; on the other hand, you are very unlikely to be able to crank your halyard up to 50 per cent of its

When you flatten the sails, sheets and halyards inevitably stretch.

breaking load, so stretch will be measured in inches rather than feet.

Sheets

Stretch is again the telling factor in a sheet, because it leads to chafe. As the load on it changes, the rope expands and contracts, and it will chafe on blocks, winch drums, shrouds and anything else it comes into contact with.

Strength is important, for obvious reasons; a bowline can reduce a rope's breaking strain by 60 per cent. If you use an oversized sheet, though, it will weigh the sail's clew down in light airs and affect its trim. Then there is ease of handling; the rope should be soft and pliable to the touch, and be winch-friendly. A stiff rope will tend to work its way out of the jaws of a self-tailer. Nor do you want a too-thin sheet, because thicker ropes are easier to handle.

A good-quality braided rope is best for sheets. Matt polyester is made up of shorter fibres spun together to give it that fuzzy feel; this makes it nice to handle and gives it good grip on a winch but

it is more elastic and not as strong as the shiny equivalent constructed from continuous filaments.

Three-strand construction can be used but it stretches more and does not lend itself to winching. It is too easily kinked. Forget about polypropylene. It is far too weak and stretchy for anything much bigger than a dayboat.

Control lines

Stretch is not as big an issue in multi-part tackles like mainsheets and kicking straps. The breaking loads are less on a rope used in a tackle, though it is worth bearing in mind that the loads on a mid-boom sheeting system are significantly higher than on end-boom sheeting. A soft, flexible construction is just as important in a rope that has to make myriad twists and turns, to help it run more freely and cut down on friction. A more loosely woven but low-stretch 8-plait construction would be better than 16-plait, which is firmer rope and not so flexible. You could use 16-plait for spinnaker uphauls and downhauls. These will be considerably shorter

◀ *You could use the same high quality, low-stretch rope for halyards, kickers and reefing lines.*

than halyards and so stretch will be less of a factor. It certainly would not be worthwhile applying one of the exotics to such mundane tasks.

Reefing lines are another matter; you want maximum strength in a light, thin line that won't chafe the sailcloth so much, so it is not worth skimping on them. On a larger cruising boat with a big mainsail it would not be excessive to use Dyneema for reefing lines, and even the mainsail outhaul. By extension, you could include the headsail roller reefing line in that, because it's another line you don't want breaking in a blow.

A word of caution, though. Because of their low stretch, exotics can be hard on deck gear. The lack of 'give' in the rope makes for excessive shock loadings as the sail collapses and fills. Exploding blocks and stripped rope clutches are routine on big racing yachts and they use far stronger sheet cars and turning blocks than the average cruising yacht. Clutches especially can suffer from the unforgiving nature of exotics. People who replace,

say, a 12mm polyester halyard with 8mm Dyneema usually find that the clutch can't grip the rope as well; the clutch grips the cover but not the core, which creeps under the sustained load. One way around this is to have a rigger fit an extra length of braided cover on the part of the halyard that goes through the clutch. Breaking strain is another consideration that needs some thought when working out rope sizes. Synthetic ropes are incredibly strong but in general it is best to err on the side of caution and leave a greater safety margin, bearing in mind that the loads on a sheet or halyard increase by the square of the wind speed; the load is four times greater in 30 knots than at 15 knots, for instance.

Value for money

For the average cruising yacht, where weight aloft is not the consideration it is on lightly rigged racing boats or some of the more extreme cruiser-racers, there is little to be gained by spending a lot of money on exotic ropes. Rope makers are only to happy to discuss the merits of their products and most will admit that their top-of-the-line polyester braids are entirely adequate for the needs of a cruising yacht. If budget is not a consideration, by all means treat the boat to Dyneema or Vectran halyards, sheets, and spinnaker guys. Otherwise, buy the best polyester you can afford, especially for halyards and reefing lines.

Rope sizes and breaking strains (given in kg)

Diameter	6mm	8mm	10mm	12mm	14mm	16mm
Dyneema	1800	3200	4200	5700	7800	9500
Braid on braid	1230	2000	2550	4000	6000	7250

16
Troubleshooting

There's too much weather helm...

That leech doesn't look right...

My sails are too baggy...

Getting rid of creases

Get the camera out

As sails age they change shape and lose some of their efficiency. Combine this with a rig that perhaps isn't set up as well as it might be, and you've got a boat that won't perform to her full potential. This leads to the temptation to spend a lot of money on new sails, when a few simple adjustments or repairs might see the old ones lasting a few more seasons. Here are a few pointers on how to troubleshoot common sail and rig problems.

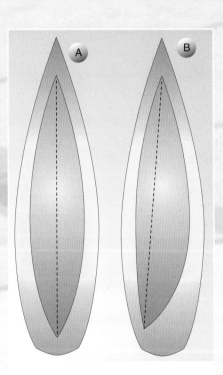

Balance depends, to a large extent, on the shape of the immersed hull when it heels. In simple terms, the less symmetrical it is, the heavier the helm.

There's too much weather helm...

Eliminating weather helm completely is rarely possible, and never desirable. It is the offspring of the relationship between the hull's centre of lateral resistance (CLR), which is the midpoint of the boat's underwater surfaces, and the sailplan's centre of effort (CE) or, more specifically, the distance between them.

Most modern cruising yacht hulls will turn into the wind when they're heeled over. The underwater shape becomes asymmetrical and the water flowing past it pushes the bow up to weather. To counteract this, a slight opposite turning force is applied with the rudder so that in effect, when you are sailing upwind, you're always steering the boat away from the wind.

As long as it is controllable, weather helm is a good thing and most boats are designed to carry some. A rudder that just trails along behind the boat contributes nothing to sailing efficiency, but one angled to push the boat downwind generates lift. The waterflow is faster on one side of the rudder than the other and, since the keel also has lift, the two work together to get the boat sailing closer to the wind – just like a genoa/mainsail combination.

Generally between 3 and 5 degrees of weather helm is considered about right. This is easy to gauge with a tiller but if you have a wheel-steered boat you will have to mark the wheel with a Turk's Head or some tape. If there is more than 5 degrees of weather helm, the rudder's lift becomes drag, the boat goes slower, and steering becomes hard work. A boat should be designed to sail perfectly balanced under full sail up to a certain

Adjusting the sail plan can affect the boat's behaviour.
(A) With the centre of effort (CE) behind the hull's centre of lateral resistance (CLR), the boat will have weather helm and try to round up into the wind.
(B) With the CE in front of the CLR, the boat will do exactly the opposite (lee helm).
(C) With the CE in line with the CLR, the helm should be neutral when sailing to windward.

Sailpower

The angle of the rudder blade shows how the helmsman compensates for weather helm. If the load on the wheel is too great, let the mainsail down the traveller track, or take in a reef.

wind speed and angle of heel. If you're out in conditions which should be the optimum for your boat – say about 12-15 knots over the deck, heeled no more than 15 degrees or so – and you've got the tiller pulled up to your chest or half a turn on the wheel to keep the boat on course, that's excessive weather helm and you need to do something about it.

The most common cause of excess weather helm is the CE of the sailplan being located too far aft. A reef in the mainsail will usually take care of that problem, but you may be merely curing the symptom, and not the cause. Instead, it might be possible to carry full sail into a higher wind range simply by making a few adjustments to the rig and sail controls. For instance, a mast that is raked too far aft is a prime cause of weather helm because it brings the CE aft. Rake is relatively easy to experiment with; on a masthead-rigged boat with a deck-stepped mast, changing rake merely involves easing the backstay and taking up on the forestay, adjusting the lower shrouds to suit. (Be careful, though – rake the mast too far forward and you'll end up with lee helm, which is infinitely less desirable than weather helm.) It is a little more complicated on a fractionally-rigged boat, where the backstay does not play such a large part in keeping the mast upright.

Is the back part of the mainsail too full? This can cause the boat to heel more than it should, which increases weather helm. Try moving the draft forward by tensioning the halyard – and the cunningham tackle, if you have one – and flatten the lower part of the sail by tightening the outhaul. The fullest part of the sail should be forward of the midpoint line between the head and the centre of the foot. On a fractionally-rigged boat, harden up on the backstay to bend the mast and flatten the sail.

The sail may be sheeted in too hard; if the leech is curved to windward, ease the sheet. An open leech will twist off to leeward and decrease the heeling force. Try easing the main down the traveller until it just starts to backwind – remember the cardinal rule of sail trim, 'if in doubt, ease it out'. This should straighten up the boat a little more and ease the pressure on the helm.

The boat's trim can also affect its balance. If the boat is down at the bows, not unusual in hull with fine bow sections where water tankage in the forepeak combines with the weight of ground tackle and cruising stores, the CLR will move forward relative to the CE and weather helm will increase.

Finally, there may be little you can do that doesn't involve more-or-less drastic surgery. Some boats are renowned for weather helm and owners have been driven to have the mainsail cut down, or add short bowsprits to move the CE forward.

That leech doesn't look right...

Mainsail

A common mainsail problem is a hooked leech, ie it curls to windward, disrupting the airflow and slowing the boat. The reason may be as simple as an over-enthusiastically tensioned leechline, or the tabling

▼ *Learn how to use your leechline and your sail will last longer.*

(construction) of the leech itself may be too tight. If the sail is poorly built, the entire leech may angle to weather for some distance. On short-battened sails you may see a crease running down the sail past the forward ends of the battens. With full battens, you may see the leech curl inwards between the batten tips. If this is the case, the sail will need some surgery.

Most of the time, though, abuse of the leechline is at fault. Usually it will have been tensioned to stop the leech fluttering in a blow, and then you'll have forgotten to ease it when the wind moderates, in which case it will cause the leech to hook to windward in lighter airs. The moral is, play with your leechline constantly.

If you have persistent problems with leech flutter, it usually means the leech is too slack. Sometimes more halyard tension or hardening up on the kicker will cure this; if not, get the sail looked at by a sailmaker. Maybe there's too much roach, which can be trimmed a little, or the seams need tightening.

Genoa

A hooked leech on a headsail affects both its performance and that of the mainsail, because it's one of the prime causes of the mainsail back-winding when going to weather. This disturbs the airflow over the lee side of the mainsail. The causes are, again, tight leechline or tight tabling. If your headsail leech is fluttering, try moving the sheet car forward to flatten the upper part of the sail before you attack the leech-line. And if you've tightened the leechline on the wind, don't forget to ease it when you come off the wind.

If the sail has been carried in too much wind and has been 'blown out', the flow will have come aft as the cloth stretches, and this will make the leech hook to windward, causing drag and sideways thrust. If extra halyard tension fails to move the draft forward, it's time to see your sailmaker.

▲ *If your sails are too full they may have 'blown out'; a recut may get you another season or two*

My sails are too baggy...

If your sails look too full, go through the rig check process (see chapter 2) before giving up and making your sailmaker a wealthier man. A badly-tuned rig means sails won't be setting properly; a sagging forestay can make a perfectly good genoa look as if it's been around the world, while a mast that leans to one side can result in a decidedly odd set to the mainsail.

Another common cause is shrinkage of the sail's luff rope. These tend to contract over time, which means the luff can't be stretched the way it was intended to be. It may be fine in light airs but can't be flattened as the wind gets up. Wrinkling along the luff that doesn't disappear as the halyard is tensioned is a sure sign that there are problems with the luff rope. This is an easy repair job for a sailmaker.

If, having gone through the rig check process, and experimented with halyard and outhaul tension, you decide that the mainsail really is too full, it still may be repairable. If the bagginess is mainly in the

▶ *Creases at the clew might mean that the sailcloth has stretched.*

forward sections a sailmaker can often sort the problem out relatively easily. If the after sections are too full – which often results from the sail being carried unreefed in strong winds – it's not quite so simple. This could involve a major recut.

Often the bottom panel on a crosscut roller furling genoa will be fuller than those above it. A prime cause of this is failure to move the sheet leads forward as the headsail is reefed, then grinding the sheet hard on. The sailcloth along the foot stretches and eventually will be permanently deformed. The remedy is to have the bottom panel replaced and practise strict sheet lead discipline thenceforth.

Getting rid of creases

To someone who takes pride in getting a boat to perform as well as possible, the sight of ugly creases in the sails is infuriating. They've led to many sails being prematurely scrapped, when the problem may have been something as simple as an out-of-tune rig or poor sail trim.

Mainsails

Creases radiating from the clew of a mainsail could indicate that the material has stretched and hardened over the years and is ready for the skip. Usually, though, it signifies that there is too much mast bend for the conditions; if the creases disappear when the wind gets up, then this is almost certainly the culprit.

Unfortunately, it's not always that simple. Creases that run up the luff or leech of a mainsail, or past the inboard end of short battens, could be caused by any number of factors and you'll have to go through a process of elimination to pin down the reasons.

Some of these factors are fairly easy to spot and to deal with. Too much halyard tension in light airs will cause a vertical crease along the luff, and that's easily remedied by easing the halyard. If the crease runs from the clew to the middle of the sail, try hardening up on the halyard and/or the cunningham. Check that the clew isn't too far above the boom. The bottom of the clew ring should be in line with the foot of the sail and if it is allowed to rise too far, then creasing will almost certainly result. If there is no metal slug to hold the clew ring hard against the track on the boom, then lash the ring down.

Insufficient batten tension, especially on fully-battened sails, can also cause creasing and this is also simple to check and cure with some advice from your sailmaker.

If none of this has any effect then it's time to get out your cheque-book. The sail could be blown out – the material stretched beyond repair – or the after part of the foot may have been cut too full, in which case the sail will need recutting or restitching.

Creases that originate from the headboard aren't easily cured, except by a sailmaker. The stitching around the board may be too tight, or the lead from the halyard attachment at the board to the sheave may be too acute. Sometimes, where there is a choice, moving the halyard to the after hole in the headboard will have an effect.

You may also see horizontal creases along the luff, which you should be able to trim out by tensioning the halyard. Persistent creases can usually be traced to sail slides sticking in the track or to shackles and seizings that aren't all identical, which will pull part of the luff out of alignment. Slides should be attached loosely, so they don't bind.

Headsails

If the sail is tacked down too far abaft the forestay, you'll see creases emanating from the spot where it enters the headfoil or from the first hank. This is easily fixed by making the tack fast further forward. A partially furled headsail often shows creases radiating from tack and head; this indicates that the middle portion of the sail is too full. Often, this results from keeping too much tension on the jibsheet when furling the sail. Letting the sail feather gently when rolling it will usually get rid of the creases.

Creases starting at a headsail clew are also common. They are a by-product of all heavy stitching around the clew and should disappear as the wind increases. A slack forestay can also accentuate any tendency towards creasing. If the sheet leads are too far aft, you may see creasing at both head and clew.

◁ *A headsail sometimes develops creases at the tack because there was too much tension when it was reefed.*

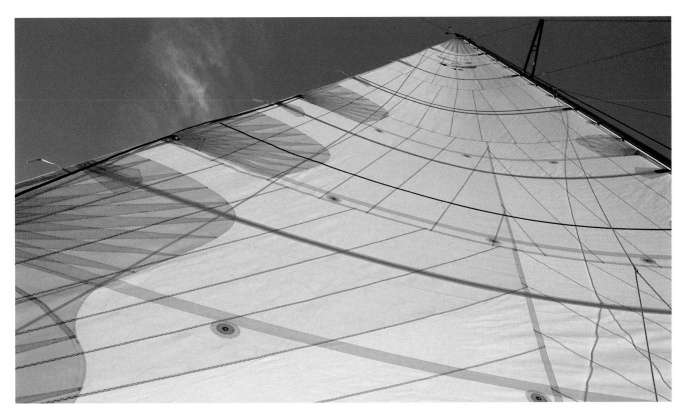

▲ *Looking upwards and analysing the shape of the sail and watching the tell-tales can tell you exactly what is going on. Few cruisers will have a mainsail that looks as good as this one though!*

Get the camera out

How do you know when it's time for a new sail wardrobe? Many sails that are junked still have a few years of life left in them. Sailmakers can do amazing things with sails that appear to be shot. Mains and genoas can be recut at considerably less cost than a replacement, and a tired old mainsail can often be rejuvenated by retro-fitting full-length battens.

The sailmaker should be able to tell on inspection whether there's still enough life left in the sailcloth to make a recut worthwhile, but to get an idea of the general set of the sails, he will either have to come sailing with you – and that will cost you – or he'll need some good photos of the sails.

Put the boat on the wind, trim the sails as you usually would, and take some shots of the mainsail looking up the mast, from halfway along the boom, to illustrate the amount of camber and its location. If you also measure the fore-and-aft diameter of the mast, the sailmaker will be able to work out the amount of mast bend. If you can, get the Windex in the shot to show the wind angle. Take some more photos looking up the leech from the end of the boom.

Lie down on the foredeck or squat down by the furling drum and take some more shots looking up the headsail luff. This will show the amount of forestay sag. Make sure the middle of the sail is in some of the shots. Go back to the mast and take some shots up the slot: between headsail and mainsail. Photograph the clews of both sails, the tacks, the headsail sheet lead, and the mainsheet traveller. Jot down the wind strength. Now put a few rolls in the genoa and take some more photos looking up the luff, along the foot, and of the sheet leads.

As well as being invaluable for troubleshooting, the photographs will stand you in good stead when the time comes to order new sails.

17 Sailcare

Damage limitation

Sail care under way

Cleaning sails

Furling problems

Polyester cloth is a tough, long-lasting material that really only has two enemies: sunlight and chafe. Unfortunately, both are in abundance during the course of the season. There is not a lot you can do to ward off the effects of ultraviolet light except to make sure the mainsail cover is always in place when you're not using the boat and to check that the sacrificial strip on the leech and foot of a roller genoa is in good condition.

Chafe is another matter altogether. This insidious creature likes to nibble at parts of the sail such as stitching, reef patches, batten pockets and the leech tabling. If you've had the sails valeted over the winter the sailmaker should have passed an eagle eye over all these bits. If not, have a really close look at them yourself. This is best done with the sail spread out on the back lawn. If the mainsail is still on the boat drop it out of its luff groove or track, leaving it on the boom. Then you can push the material over the boom as you inspect it. Look for broken or worn stitching and stretched stitch holes – these mean the seam will be weak. You shouldn't be able to see daylight through any of the seams.

It's important to repair damaged stitching quickly, as even a few broken stitches can become a lot of broken stitches – and possibly a luff-to-leech tear – towards the end of a hard season. If your own needlework is of the ham-fisted variety you could always plead with the local loft to repair the sail, but don't count on them having time to do it at the start of the season when most of them are flat-out.

The hardware also needs a close look. Sail slides can come under a lot of strain, especially at the headboard and tack where loads are highest. Sailmakers recommend doubling up the sail slides in these areas. The top slide should be free to articulate, or the headboard will tend to jam on its way up the mast. Slides in general need to be checked regularly. UV light degrades the plastic and this can be spotted easily enough – the plastic gets discoloured. The webbing attaching the slides to the sail tends to wear and fray but is easy enough to replace. Some slides are held on with shackles and these have a tendency to go missing in the dead of night, so a good supply of spares should be kept on board. Many fully-battened sails have expensive and complex devices for attaching the batten ends to the luff car. If they fall apart they're difficult to bodge up, so at least one of these should be added to the spares box.

Check the headboard for worn or corroded rivets and eyelets, and have a good look at the luff wire and the clew and tack rings. These are

Plastic rollers on the shrouds can reduce headsail chafe.

MERIDIAN SAILING SCHOOL

Sailpower

high-stress areas and although they're strongly built they also suffer from general wear and tear.

Damage limitation

Mainsails chafe more than headsails, because more parts of them come into contact with the rigging. The knifelike trailing edges of spreaders are prime culprits. These 'aerodynamically efficient' spreader shapes were developed for racing yachts and have since found their way onto all too many cruising boats, where they're nothing but a nuisance – they don't make one iota of difference to performance on a typical cruiser but they do harm sails. You can offset the damage by putting spreader patches on the sail. On long voyages where a fair amount of time is spent reaching or running with the main eased against the spreaders, it pays to tape split hosepipe or pipe lagging over the spreader edges.

The main bears on the cap and/or aft lower shrouds much of the time, and while they fret merrily away at the sailcloth in general they will rub through full-length batten pockets in short order. Sticky-back dacron patches will help in the short term, but a more permanent cure is to get a sailmaker to sew nylon webbing along the pockets. It always pays to keep a close eye on batten pockets because they lead a pretty hard life, especially on short-battened sails where there is a lot of flogging when reefing.

It's a good idea to fit full-length plastic rollers on shrouds that come into contact with sails. Dyform rigging wire, with its sharp corners, is especially hard on stitching and sailcloth. Some long-distance cruisers fit lengths of garden hose over the shrouds for downwind passages and throw them away when they get to their destination. Another blue-water dodge to avoid chafe is to fit plastic hose over reefing lines where they pass over the folds of the reefed sail, but this verges on overkill for the average coastal cruiser.

Other lines that cause chafe over the long term are lazyjacks and the topping lift, which tend to rub across the proud stitching on the seams. You can go some way toward preventing this by rigging the lazyjacks so they can be taken forward to the mast while under sail, and adjusting the topping lift so it doesn't rub against the leech.

A headsail suffers a little damage each time it is tacked. As it's dragged from one side of the boat to the other it chafes against shrouds, spreaders, mast or babystay. As with the mainsail, any part that stands clear of the sailcloth is vulnerable, especially the stitching. The parts of the sail that come into contact with the rig should be checked during the season, so it would pay to drop the genoa on deck once in a while and examine the stitching along the leech.

Damage limitation is simple enough. Make sure the sail has chafe patches where it bears against the spreader tips, and along its foot where it passes over the pulpit or guardrails. Spreader tips can be covered with inexpensive plastic caps from chandlers or you can go all salty and make up some leather protectors.

Go around the foredeck and tape up all split pins and anything else that can snag or tear the sail. The forward lifeline bottlescrews should

It pays to check your sails regularly for signs of wear and tear.

1 UV degradation has ruined this furling genoa's sacrificial strip.
2 Mildew has formed and there is a missing grommet.
3 Wear and tear on the head of a genoa.
4 The webbing attaching the slides has started to wear.
5 The effects of too much halyard tension.

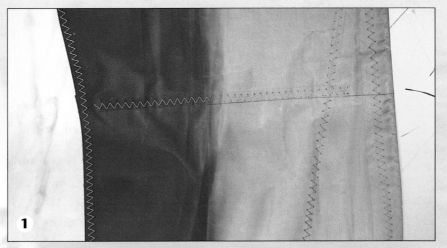

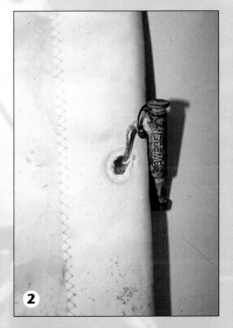

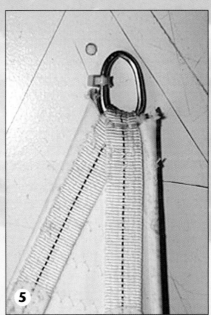

be completely taped up so they don't chafe or bleed grease onto the sail. Either tape up the shroud bottlescrews or fit plastic covers (make sure the covers are loose enough not to trap dirt and water inside). Check wire halyards and lifelines for broken strands.

Sail care under way

Most drivers develop a sense of mechanical sympathy – they come to recognise the agonised sounds an engine makes when it's being over-revved or is in too high a gear for the speed. The ability to empathise with sails is not so easily acquired, which is one reason why sailmakers will never be short of repair business.

Step one is to not let the sails flog. Flogging is bad news, because it breaks down the filler which is put into the sailcloth to stabilise the weave and stop it from stretching. Once this is gone, so is the ability of the sail to retain its shape. This will happen over a period of years in any case but there is no reason to speed up the process.

On short-batten mainsails, the cloth immediately in front of the batten pockets is usually the first to suffer the effects of flogging, which results in a noticeable 'hinge' effect. Eventually the Dacron fibres will break down. Fully-battened mains are much better in this regard. When you're reefing the main, rather than dumping the sheet altogether and letting the sail flog madly, try to spill just enough wind to take the weight out of it so you can drag the luff down easily.

Leech flutter in the sails might be mildly annoying to the crew but when it's prolonged it can gradually destroy the sailcloth. The noisy, rapidfire flutter known as 'motorboating' which often occurs when the headsail is strapped hard in for a beat is especially damaging. Don't be afraid to tension up the leechline to get rid of this horrid noise, but don't forget to ease it off when you come off the wind.

There is a lamentable tendency to treat sheet leads as if the cars were bolted in place. It's all too common to see boats blithely sailing along with the bottom half of the genoa trimmed correctly while the upper part of the leech is flogging away, out of the crew's sight. This can be avoided by using the sheet leads correctly – moving them forward as

▲ If you don't have covers on your bottlescrews, make sure that all pins that could snag sheets or sails are taped over.

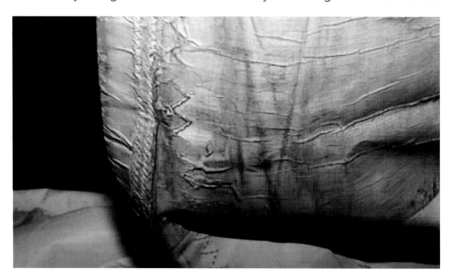

◀ The spreader patch has done its job.

▶ Baggywrinkles – the traditional answer to chafe, but too 'retro' for modern yachts.

▼ Here's a neat trick to stop your sheets from getting snagged on the bottlescrews.

the headsail is reefed, and also when the boat is put on to a reach. If they're too far forward on a beat, you'll be stretching the leech, and if too far aft, there will be too much strain on the foot.

When you're tacking, release the lee sheet early enough so the sail doesn't catch against the spreader as the boat comes about, and sheet in quickly to minimise flogging. Don't trim the genoa in so hard that it rests against the spreader – three or four inches off is usually enough when going to windward.

Lastly, don't overtension halyards. They should be just tight enough to get the horizontal wrinkles out of the sail. If vertical creases appear the luff tension is too high and if repeated often enough such abuse can deform the sail. When you leave the boat, ease off the genoa halyard and the main outhaul; leaving tension on them can result in permanent stretch in the boltropes.

Sailpower

Cleaning sails

Many of us leave this job to the sailmakers as part of the valeting process, and their big industrial washing machines certainly provide the least labour-intensive way of cleaning a season's grime off the sails. But there's no reason why stains can't be tackled on the spot, as it were.

Polyester sailcloth is pretty tough, and shrugs off attacks from most chemicals, so stains from blood, rust or mildew won't hurt the sails – they just look bad. There are assorted home-grown concoctions for rust stains but why not do what the sailmakers do and use a proprietary treatment like Coppings Rust Remover, which contains hydrofluoric acid. As well as getting the rust out it will remove anything else with iron in it, like blood, and is also good for cleaning off residue from oxidised aluminium.

Mildew

Mildew is a little trickier and once it gets a firm hold in between the fibres it's very difficult to remove. Even if you kill the spores the stains may well remain. You need to attack mildew as soon as you spot it, because it will spread quickly. About the only thing that will shift it is bleach, which is the prime constituent of most commercial mildew removers. If you can't find any of these in the shops, you can make up a solution yourself from Chlorox bleach – about a cupful to a bucket of water. Neat bleach won't harm polyester but could turn it yellow. You may have to soak particularly stubborn stains in the bleach solution overnight. (Never use bleach on nylon or Kevlar sails – it will eat them away.)

With mildew, prevention is much easier than the cure. The spores love damp and dirt so make sure your sails are clean and dry; during the winter, keep them somewhere where air can circulate around them. In the sailing season, wash your sails down with fresh water once in a while to clean off salt and airborne grime. Salt crystals are small but sharp and they will eventually slice through the tiny fibres that make up polyester yarn. They also make the sail heavier and this is especially noticeable in spinnakers that have been dunked in the sea. As well as that, salt attracts moisture, and moisture attracts mildew – though, oddly, mildew does not flourish on salt-laden surfaces.

Furling problems

Like domestic fridges or washing machines, modern headsail furling gears are so reliable that we take them for granted. When something does go wrong the awakening is rude and the inconvenience huge. If they're installed according to the maker's instructions, maintained properly and operated with a little common sense, furling gears should give little trouble. But if you throw a careless rigger, an inexperienced owner or crew, or a healthy dose of Murphy's Law into the equation, all sorts of interesting things can happen.

Sometimes the gear will display a reluctance to unfurl when you are trying to make sail. Before reaching for the winch handle, take a look

SAIL REPAIR KIT

It doesn't matter whether you're coastal cruising or heading off across the Atlantic, one day you will appreciate being able to repair your sails, even if only in the form of a temporary bodge to get you home. A basic repair kit doesn't cost much to put together. The following list should cover most emergencies.

• **Palm** If you buy both right and left-handed types then no one will have an excuse not to help repair a sail.
• **Tools** A decent pair of scissors, pliers, a hammer, grommets and punches and Stanley knife. A battery- or butane-powered hot knife is very useful for heat-sealing sailcloth so it doesn't fray, and also for cutting lines.
• **Needles** Smear them with vaseline and keep in an airtight container. One of those patent hand-stitchers will come in handy should you ever need to sew a long seam back together. (I once spent the best part of a ten-day voyage sewing sails, so I speak from the heart). If not, use an awl

to pre-punch the holes for the needle.
• **Twine** A couple of rolls of light and heavy sailmaker's thread, preferably waxed, and a couple of different grades of whipping twine.
• **Sticky-back dacron** This stuff is invaluable. Buy plenty of it. You can use it to hold the cloth together while it's being stitched, or on its own for chafe patches or quick and easy get-you-home repairs.
• **Sailcloth** Ask your sailmaker for a few offcuts in various weights.
• **Sail slides** Pack a handful of these for a long voyage. Plastic slides have a habit of failing due to chafe. Don't forget the small plastic shackles that connect full battens to the slides – they have a habit of disappearing at sea.
• **Webbing** Light nylon webbing is useful for reinforcing edges or corners of sails or for affixing sail slides.
• **Tape** Buy lots of it. Self-amalgamating tape, duct tape, spinnaker repair tape, electrical tape (for chafe protection).

The essential tools: a needle and palm (above) is still the most vital part of any sail repair kit (below).

up the foretriangle; the genoa halyard may have wrapped itself once or twice around the forestay. The usual cause of 'halyard wrap' is a genoa that's short in the luff so there is too much halyard exposed between masthead sheave and top swivel. One cure is to fit a halyard restrainer a few inches below the sheave and lead the halyard down through that before attaching it to the swivel. Another is to fit a pennant between head of the sail and swivel, to bring the latter closer to the sheave. As long as the angle between headfoil and halyard is 10 degrees or so, the halyard should not wrap.

Many modern boats, especially performance cruisers, have full-hoist headsails that keep a minimal distance and a good angle between sheave and swivel, so halyard wrap is not as common as it used to be. When it does occur, it's usually down to inadequate halyard tension, which is something to bear in mind if you've been sailing in light airs with the halyard eased.

If spinnaker or second genoa halyards are kept clipped to the bow pulpit, make sure they're well tensioned or they can all too easily become caught up in the sail as it's being furled, causing another head-scratching moment.

Sailpower

What if there is no sign of halyard wrap, but the gear still won't turn? If the sail is set, the most likely suspect is a riding turn on the furling drum. These can be relatively easy to sort out, unless you've tried to winch in the furling line at the first sign of resistance, and thereby made matters worse. A spell perched on a heaving bow (these things never happen on a calm day) while digging into a snarled furling drum with a spike will hammer a simple lesson into the hardest of heads; when unrolling the sail, especially in any kind of a breeze, keep some tension on the furling line by surging it around a winch.

The chances of a riding turn can be further cut by ensuring that the furling line exits the drum at a right angle to the forestay; the first lead block should be positioned as close to the drum as possible. If the lead is right the line shouldn't pile up on itself around the drum. I've seen a riding turn jammed so solidly the line had to be cut off the drum, which is a good reason to keep a spare furling line on board.

A forestay that's too loose is another possible cause of sticky furling gear; the resulting vibration and shaking about can damage the foil extrusions or loosen their connections, and the headfoil will flop from side to side as it turns. In the interests of good sailing performance it is essential to have the rig tuned properly, and if the boat has a backstay adjuster, don't be afraid to use it.

While the situations outlined above are rare provided the relevant precautions are taken, the fact remains that many furling systems are harder to operate than they need to be. It should be possible to roll up a well set-up system by hand in most conditions. The need to winch in a furling line in anything below a stiff breeze is usually an indication that there is too much friction in the system. In most cases this is down to a combination of low-quality hardware and poorly thought-out deck layout.

Most production builders have to cut corners somewhere to keep costs down and inconspicuous items like stanchion-mounted furling line blocks are prime candidates for penny-pinching. Upgrading to

▲ Here the furling line has stretched in a strong breeze and the sail has not rolled up correctly.

Splinters Apprentice

◄ Sailbags on deck have become a rare sight with the advent of furling gears.

It is important that the halyard leads from furling gear swivel to the masthead sheave at the correct angle, to prevent it from wrapping around the forestay as the sail is unrolled.

roller or ball-bearing blocks that swivel to ensure the lead is always fair can make a noticeable difference.

The best furling line set-ups I've used have also been the simplest ones; led along the stanchion bases, with the last block fitted near the forward end of the cockpit, and the line taken to a cleat or dedicated winch on the coaming alongside the wheel. This means that from the helm the pull on the line is at a shallow, hence more efficient, angle, and in a strong breeze the winch can be used to help out. It also allows the helmsman to set or furl the sail without leaving the wheel. This set-up isn't practical on center cockpit boats because it means having the furling line cross the side deck.

Recently there has been a tendency for boatbuilders to lead furling lines across the foredeck and over the coachroof to a winch on the cabintop. There are a couple of fundamental flaws to this approach. First there is the folly of having a line bisecting the foredeck at the perfect height to trip someone up. Then there is the potential for chafe involved in having the line travel through and around bullseyes or deck organisers. The friction in the system almost guarantees that you will have to winch the furling line in anything more than a light breeze. There is the difficulty of making or reducing sail if you are alone in the cockpit – having to leave the wheel in order to winch in a furling line is annoying and inefficient. It takes a long time to winch in a big genoa using a small halyard winch, during which time the sail is flogging away while you juggle sheet and winch handle. It adds another line to the pile of spaghetti on the cockpit sole.

Finally, there is the potential for causing serious damage to the furling gear. Someone grinding away under a dodger cannot see the top of the sail and so will be oblivious to a halyard wrap or other problem.

One last thought – don't spare the expense when you're replacing a worn furling line. Buy a top-quality pre-stretched Dacron line or even a Spectra or Dyneema line. Just imagine how you'd feel if the furling line snapped on a dark night with the wind getting up.

Index